MW00996285

How Leaders Improve

How Leaders Improve

A Playbook for Leaders Who Want to Get Better Now

John Gates, PhD, Jeff Graddy, PhD, and
Sacha Lindekens, PhD

An Imprint of ABC-CLIO, LLC
Santa Barbara, California • Denver, Colorado

Library of Congress Cataloging-in-Publication Data

Names: Gates, John, 1962– author. | Graddy, Jeff, author. | Lindekens, Sacha, author.
Title: How leaders improve : a playbook for leaders who want to get better now / John Gates, PhD, Jeff Graddy, PhD, and Sacha Lindekens, PhD.
Description: 1 Edition. | Santa Barbara : Praeger, [2017] | Includes bibliographical references and index.
Identifiers: LCCN 2017027834 (print) | LCCN 2017030279 (ebook) | ISBN 9781440860584 (ebook) | ISBN 9781440860577 (hardcopy : alk. paper)
Subjects: LCSH: Leadership. | Communication in management.
Classification: LCC HD57.7 (ebook) | LCC HD57.7 .G3778 2017 (print) | DDC 658.4/092—dc23
LC record available at https://lccn.loc.gov/2017027834

ISBN: 978-1-4408-6057-7 (print)
ISBN: 978-1-4408-6058-4 (ebook)

21 20 19 18 17   1 2 3 4 5

This book is also available as an eBook.

Praeger
An Imprint of ABC-CLIO, LLC

ABC-CLIO, LLC
130 Cremona Drive, P.O. Box 1911
Santa Barbara, California 93116-1911
www.abc-clio.com

This book is printed on acid-free paper ∞

Manufactured in the United States of America

Contents

Preface

Imagine you have a goal of being a world-class marathon runner. Let's say you are a decent runner today and have even run a few local marathons, with respectable times, but you are not nearly good enough to win a national-level race. So, how would you go about preparing for your ultimate goal? How would you improve your racing skills so that you were running at a much higher level?

Surely you would not just read about how fast the winning runners ran in the last big race (sure they won, but how did they get that good and that fast?). Nor would you set out to review the collapse of great runners who failed to achieve their potential or "bonked" in the final mile (that may be interesting, but at best only tells you what not to do), and you certainly would not just cross your fingers and hope you somehow, miraculously outperform all of your previous non-world-class times on the day of the big race (hint: You will not lower your personal best by hoping really hard on race day). But this is what most leaders do in order to get better at leading—they read books about "great" leaders, they read cases studies on failed or flawed leaders, and in many cases they just hope that their skills as a leader will grow organically as they move up in organizations.

There is nearly an unlimited supply of books and articles on the topic of leadership, and yet most leaders find it very hard to truly improve their leadership skills because most of the wisdom on the bookshelf to date does not teach leaders HOW to actually get better. While there are plenty of books that spotlight "great" leaders, and plenty of others that share wisdom about what it takes to be a "good" or "great" leader, what makes *How Leaders Improve* different is that we have created a playbook for how any leader can get *better* in a practical, immediate way.

Because leadership is a complex phenomenon, leaders often need help to improve their leadership skills. As leadership development consultants, this is what we, the authors, have spent our careers doing, and now we want to share our research and our experience with others through an easy-to-apply book that we believe will strike a chord with any leader who reads it. That's because *How Leaders Improve,* while based on research, includes insights and practical recommendations that any leader, or anyone who aspires to be a leader, can apply right away in order to make measurable improvement in how one leads other people.

In many sports, knowing the playbook and what you need to do next helps you get better and ultimately win the game. Similarly, *How Leaders Improve* gives leaders focus, as well as confidence that taking action based on these recommendations will ensure that they achieve their leadership goals.

How Leaders Improve outlines 10 "insights" that are based on research the authors have conducted in the real world with leaders, and these insights have been boiled down so that they are easy to understand and easy to apply. The fact that these insights are real-world stories and findings derived from actual leaders in actual organizations lends street credibility to the recommendations and suggests that if a leader follows the playbook outlined in *How Leaders Improve,* that leader, too, will be able to improve significantly. So, whether you are a leader, an aspiring leader, a teacher of leadership, a leadership development professional, or an organizational decision-maker trying to ensure that your company invests wisely in its leadership development efforts, we believe this book is for you.

Acknowledgments

Many people contributed to this book, and we would like to express our sincere appreciation. First and foremost, we would like to thank our partner at Avion Consulting, Steve Williams, for his expertise, for his integrity, and for being the consummate team player. We couldn't have done this without you, Steve.

We would also like to thank our administrative assistant, Katie Keller, for her tireless work on several of the more technical aspects of this book. Thanks also to Irma Campos, Lizzy Byrd, and David Diaso for their contributions during the early aspects of this project.

If not for clients who allowed us to use data that we gathered over the course of our work with their leaders, we would not have had the basis for our study or book. So, many thanks to Mary Anderson, Jean Erath, Becky Locke, Mary Savage, and Tammy Steele for supporting our study. In addition, we express our gratitude to all of our "most improved leaders"—the clients who participated in our study and who offered their valuable time and insights into how they actually improved as leaders.

A number of colleagues outside of Avion Consulting provided wise counsel and encouragement throughout this process, and we would like to say a special thank you to Mark Ehrhart, Rob Fazio, Jackie Freiberg, Kevin Freiberg, Himanshu Kalra, and John Stenbeck.

Our excellent literary agent, Leticia Gomez, managed to help these book-publishing rookies get a base hit during our first at-bat, and for that we are very grateful. And our senior editor at Praeger, Hilary Claggett, patiently and skillfully guided us through the process of turning a manuscript into an actual book. Our sincere thanks to both of you.

Finally, of course, we would like to thank our families, whose love and support make it possible for us to do what we do. A heartfelt thanks to Lisa, Tyler, Cameron, and Lindsay; to Jenny, Ava, and Tyler; and to Laura, Taylor, and Reid. We love and appreciate you all more than we can say.

CHAPTER ONE

Why (and How) We Wrote This Book

Why We Wrote This Book

We are leadership development professionals. And while writing a book is fairly common among professionals in our field, this is the first book for any of us. In fact, one of us, when asked about the possibility of writing a book, has often joked that a lifelong goal has been to *not* write a book.

Perhaps this has been due to the lack of a burning passion to write anything. Or, perhaps it has been due to the fact that none of us has really thought we had much that was unique to contribute to the field of leadership development. After all, there are a million books out there on leadership; why add another one?

Then, a couple of years ago, a question came up in our discussions with one another, and the question turned into the idea for a study, and then a book. And since that time we have been unable to get that question out of our minds. So, we decided to abandon that lifelong goal to never write a book.

Here's the question we can't seem to get out of our minds: How do leaders improve?

This might sound like a very simple question. After all, as noted above, volumes have been written on the topic of leadership. And, in particular, much has been written on the topic of what makes leaders *good*. However, a scan of the literature on leadership reveals that surprisingly little has been written about how leaders actually get *better*. The general message in the literature tends to be: *"Here is what great leaders do; emulate these behaviors, and you too will be a great leader."* However, our experience as leadership development professionals suggests that becoming more effective as a leader is not so simple.

Take for example the high-potential leader we worked with whose career progression was being impacted by his colleagues' perceptions that he was political and overly self-interested. Although this leader didn't personally agree with these perceptions, he certainly understood that he needed to address them.

In fact, this leader took some meaningful steps to address others' concerns about him. He thanked individuals for their feedback, developed a thoughtful action plan, and made a good-faith effort to implement his action plan. However, six months later, he received a follow up 360-degree feedback report, and his feedback indicated that many colleagues continued to perceive him as political and overly self-interested. This leader, like many others who try to change their behavior, had run into predictable challenges that undermined his efforts to get better in an area in which he was seeking to improve.

An article written by leadership expert Jeffrey Pfeffer, published in the January 2016 issue of *McKinsey Quarterly,* illustrates this point:

> This consuming interest in leadership and how to make it better has spawned a plethora of books, blogs, TED talks, and commentary. Unfortunately, these materials are often wonderfully disconnected from organizational reality and, as a consequence, useless for sparking improvement. Maybe that's one reason the enormous resources invested in leadership development have produced so few results.[1]

Pfeffer goes on to cite a study indicating that somewhere between $14 billion and $50 billion is spent on leadership development each year in the United States alone.

We think Pfeffer's article makes several excellent points. First, there is indeed a wealth of information out there on leadership. Second, this information often does not focus on what leaders actually *do* in organizations. Finally, until we as leadership development professionals do a better job of connecting what leaders actually do in organizations with leadership development *results,* organizations are arguably wasting a lot of money on their leadership development efforts.

Ironically, despite the fact that Pfeffer claims, correctly in our opinion, that existing leadership development materials are largely "useless for sparking *improvement,*" the rest of this excellent article makes no mention of how leaders actually *improve.* Rather, Pfeffer's focus, like that of so many other publications on leadership, is on traits and behaviors that make leaders *good* or *bad,* not on factors that enable leaders to actually get *better.*

Because we agree with Pfeffer's premise, though, we have sought to offer a different kind of leadership book. As Pfeffer has encouraged, our study is very much connected to organizational reality. Indeed, we conducted research to learn what actual leaders in actual organizations actually do to improve their effectiveness. This book provides practical recommendations for what leaders can do to improve, what teachers of leadership can do to ensure the effectiveness of what they are teaching, and what organizations can do in order to make sure they actually get a return on their investment (ROI) from their leadership development efforts.

The inspiration for this study, in large part, was the fantastic business book *Good to Great* by Jim Collins. As we have worked with leaders in various industries around the world, we have often cited this book to illustrate key ideas related to organizational effectiveness. Almost invariably, numerous other people in whatever meeting we are in agree that it is one of their favorite business books, as well.

One of the most appealing things about *Good to Great* is that Collins did not simply state what he believes to be true about organizational effectiveness on the basis of his own experience. There are many other books out there like that, including lots of really good books. But Collins's approach was different.

Collins started with data. More specifically, he developed a data set: Companies whose performance had gone from good to great over a specific period of time, compared with other companies in the same industries whose performance had stayed flat over that same period. And then he asked the question: What's the difference? Why did some companies go from good to great, while others did not? He and his research team then went where the data led them, and the result was a book with some profound and practical insights on the topic of how companies actually improve their performance.[2]

After years of relying on the insights in *Good to Great* when working with our clients, we started to wonder: Is there a comparable book related to leadership? In other words, has a study been done that looks at *leaders* who have improved significantly in terms of some specific measure of performance and that then seeks to answer the question: How do leaders actually get better?

We have looked for such a book. We have asked other leadership development professionals if they are aware of such a book. We have had associates in academe review the literature in the field of leadership looking for such a book. And the answer is always the same: Surprisingly, there is relatively little literature out there that focuses on the question: How do leaders improve?

This is not meant in any way to be critical of the existing literature in the field of leadership. Our bookshelves and iPads are full of hundreds of excellent books on leadership, and we have frequently cited the work of other authors in our work as leadership development consultants over the past 20 years or so. And we have cited some of those excellent authors in this book.

But once it was concluded that the specific question we had in mind had not been extensively explored (at least, not using the type of approach we were thinking about), we started to feel like we actually had a *responsibility* to the field of leadership development to do this study and get any resulting insights out there. In short, we went from feeling like we would *never* write a book to feeling like we *had* to write a book.

Interestingly, while it appears that there is little if any empirical research on our specific question in the field of leadership development, a similar question has been asked and to some extent answered in other fields, including the fields of psychology, addiction treatment, elite sports performance, and weight management, to name a few. As a result, we know quite a lot about how people can improve their mental health, achieve peak athletic performance, combat addiction, and lose weight. And, in fact, we believe that much of what we know about personal improvement in these other fields can help inform our understanding of how leaders improve. Indeed, we will refer back to research from these fields later, when discussing insights from our study of leaders who have managed to change for the better over time. We hope that this book adds to the literature on "improvement" by focusing on what it takes to get better in the field of leadership.

As noted above, one type of audience we have in mind for this book is the "teacher of leadership," and for us this includes anyone from academics in a college or university context to leadership development professionals— whether one-person leadership coaching shops, management consulting firms, or leaders in organizational Learning and Development functions. We consider ourselves "teachers of leadership" (of the "management consulting firm" variety), and in our profession, people sometimes ask us if we believe "a leopard can change its spots" or a "zebra can change its stripes." What people are really asking us here is whether we think leaders can fundamentally change their character or behavior, or whether leaders are destined to perpetually demonstrate the same basic attributes.

In our experience, people rarely if ever change their fundamental character. And, in fact, we believe that we, as leadership development professionals, ought *not* be about the business of trying to get a leader to fundamentally change his or her stripes (for example, trying to coach a leader to change an innate aspect of his or her very personality). However, people certainly do grow, evolve, mature, and change their behaviors. We have seen countless examples of this in our work with leaders, and in fact our mission as leadership development professionals is to partner with leaders in order to unleash the potential within them—which almost inherently involves growth, evolution, maturation, and behavior change.

To summarize, the purpose of this book is not to share our point of view about what good leadership looks like, nor is it to make an argument for what it takes for a leader to achieve a change in terms of his or her fundamental makeup or character. Rather, the focus of this book is to share with you, our reader, a number of insights based on research into the question: How do leaders actually get better as leaders?

After all, as noted above, billions of dollars are spent on leadership development initiatives each year. And, although participants in these leadership development efforts often report valuing the experience, demonstrating the ROI can be very hard. In short, we believe that adopting the approaches highlighted by our research can serve to improve the effectiveness of our leadership development efforts and enhance the ROI on these leadership development initiatives.

We'd like to make one final point about *why* we wrote this book before moving onto the question of *how* we wrote this book. Once we had completed our study, analyzed our data, and come up with an initial set of insights, we had a realization: Even though our study was done with a number of organizations in the corporate context, we believe the insights and recommendations highlighted in this book are relevant to *all* leaders, whether in commercial enterprises, not-for-profit organizations, academic institutions, sports teams, or any other context in which people lead (which is to say, in *any* context). So, our hope is that through the 10 insights into "how leaders improve" offered throughout this book, as well as the practical recommendations at the end of each of the next 10 chapters, leaders and those who develop leaders will have a new playbook in order to take their game to the next level.

How We Wrote This Book

As mentioned above, the inspiration for this book, at least in part, was the excellent business book *Good to Great* by Jim Collins. More specifically, our goal in embarking on this study was to use an approach that was analogous to Collins's, but at the leader level rather than the organization level.

As any leadership development professional knows, one of the most basic forms of data we work with is 360-degree feedback. This refers to a process in which direct reports, peers, one's manager (or managers), and potentially others provide feedback to a leader through an anonymous survey. The survey categories and questions are often based on a given organization's competency model or some other framework that represents what a given organization expects its leaders to be good at.

A 360-degree feedback process is sometimes used as a stand-alone process, and it is sometimes used as part of a larger leadership development process. For example, it is not uncommon for leaders within a given organization to participate in a leadership development program consisting of 360-degree feedback, leadership training, one-on-one leadership coaching, and other types of leadership development activities.

The goal of all of this, of course, is to help leaders improve. For leaders who are already good (for example, an organization's "high-potential, high-performing" leaders), the goal is to take these leaders and help them to become even more effective. For leaders who are going through some sort of transition (for example, to a bigger leadership role), the goal is to ensure that these leaders have the skills necessary to be effective in their new role. And, frankly, sometimes leaders end up in such programs because they are struggling and need some help. But in any case, the goal is to help leaders improve.

For a long time when we did this sort of work, we would include a 360-degree feedback assessment up front, provide lots of training and coaching, and conclude at the end of it all that the leaders must have improved. But we are embarrassed to admit that we generally didn't have any real data to support the claim that the leaders we had been working with had actually gotten any better.

So, more recently, we have become somewhat insistent that if we are going to use a 360-degree feedback assessment at the start of a leadership development effort, then we should use a similar assessment at the end of the effort to find out: Did these leaders actually improve?

Of course, this raises another question: Has a leader really improved just because people completing a survey say he or she has improved? This may seem like a fairly straightforward question. However, in our view, this question gets at the very essence of leadership. The short answer, in our humble opinion, is: Yes. A leader really has improved just because people completing a survey say he or she has improved.

Here's the somewhat longer answer. Paul Gaske, a long-time mentor, colleague, and friend of ours, was a thought leader in the area of leader credibility. Among many other things, Dr. Gaske taught us two important things about leader credibility.

First, credibility is a perceived phenomenon. A leader cannot *be* credible; rather, people whom one seeks to lead can only *perceive* a leader as more or less credible. As we sometimes tell groups of leaders we work with, being a leader is a little bit like being a stand-up comedian. If *you* think you're hysterical, but the *audience* isn't laughing, the audience is sort of right by definition. Similarly, if you think you're a great leader, but the people you seek to lead don't think so, they are sort of right by definition. When it comes to leader credibility, perception *is* reality. Or, as the late, great management thinker Peter Drucker put it, "There is no definition of 'leader' other than one who has followers."

The second thing Dr. Gaske taught us about leader credibility is that it *matters.* To support this point, we turn to another of the great business books: *The Service Profit Chain* by Heskett, Sasser, and Schlesinger.[3]

These three Harvard Business School professors started with the question: What makes companies profitable? Through their research, they found that the most significant driver of profitability is customer or client retention. They then asked: What drives retention? They found that the biggest driver of retention was service quality and value.

So, you guessed it, they then asked: What drives service quality and value? They found that the biggest driver of service quality and value was employee satisfaction. And this groundbreaking research led to many other books and even more articles on this set of relationships, not to mention countless employee surveys (a few of which have been done by us and our colleagues over the years).

Surprisingly, though, the Service Profit Chain researchers did not pose one additional, critical question (or, at least, the answer to this additional question did not explicitly appear in the model they developed). To us, this additional, critical question is: What drives employee satisfaction—or its more progressive cousin, employee engagement?

Others, however, have addressed this question. For example, both Zenger and Folkman (the *Extraordinary Leader*)[4] and Buckingham and Coffman (*First, Break all the Rules*)[5] cited research indicating that a significant driver of employee engagement—in fact, maybe the *biggest* driver— is employees' satisfaction with their immediate leader. And, of course, satisfaction—like credibility—is a matter of perception. And perception is exactly what is measured with a 360-degree feedback survey.

So, we have established two things. First, leader credibility is important— it really does help drive outcomes such as profitability. Second, leader credibility is largely driven by perception.

All of which leads back to our question: How do leaders really improve? More specifically: When a leader is perceived as having become much more effective over time, what tends to account for that improvement?

In order to answer that question, we identified groups of leaders from three different organizations, each in a different industry. In each case, these leaders went through a 360-degree feedback process, followed by some steps to help the leader improve (coaching, training, and so on).

A part of the process in each case was the development of an action plan in which the leader identified strengths, areas for development, and action steps. In addition, each leader identified four or five 360-degree survey items that best represented the areas that he or she would be working on over the course of the ensuing six- to nine-month period. Toward the end of this period (during which many of our participants were involved in a leadership development program—meaning coaching and training), the leaders went through a second round of 360-degree feedback. This time, however, the 360-degree survey was a shorter and slightly adapted version of the full-blown survey that was used at the outset. To begin with, this follow-up survey included two new items:

- This individual has consistently worked to address areas for development based on his/her 360-degree feedback
- This individual has demonstrated improvement in overall leadership effectiveness since receiving his/her 360-degree feedback

For each of these two items, the following scale was used:

1 = Strongly Disagree
2 = Disagree
3 = Neither Agree Nor Disagree
4 = Agree
5 = Strongly Agree

The point of these two survey items, of course, was to give participants some rich feedback related to a couple of questions. Beyond these two general survey items, each leader was also surveyed on just the four to five items that he or she had identified early in the action planning process, based on his or her areas for development from the initial 360-degree survey.

In short, this brief follow-up survey was meant to answer three questions. First, did the people with whom a given leader works perceive that the leader had actually been working on improving as a leader? Second, did those people conclude that the leader actually had gotten better as a leader in general? And third, did those people conclude that the leader actually had gotten better in the specific areas that the leader had identified as his or her areas of focus throughout the program?

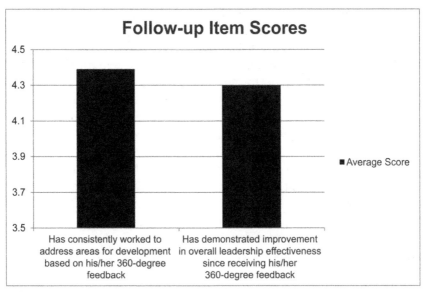

Figure 1.1

One interesting finding when looking at the results of these follow-up surveys is that nearly *all* leaders participating in these leadership development programs were perceived as having worked on his or her areas for development, and as having improved at least somewhat in terms of overall leadership effectiveness, as Figure 1.1 illustrates.

We think this represents very good news for organizations that invest in well-designed, effectively implemented leadership development programs. Simply put, if perceived leader effectiveness really does drive business results, as argued above, and if leaders participating in well-crafted leadership efforts really are seen as improving, then it follows that when organizations make this investment, it is money (and time and energy) well spent.

Having said that, the primary point of this study is not to determine whether leadership development programs in general (or even particular leadership development programs) actually result in increased leadership effectiveness. Rather, the primary point of this study is to find out what the *most improved* leaders *actually do* in order to get better.

To address this question, we needed to make a decision about how to identify our sample of leaders. Before getting into our specific method, which is actually rather simple, it would perhaps be helpful for us to clarify a couple of principles we sought to adhere to.

First, we decided that we wanted our study to be one that would be help-ful to three key audiences: Actual and aspiring leaders, those who teach and coach leaders and aspiring leaders (whether in an academic or a corporate environment), and those who make investment decisions related to leadership development. In other words, we decided we did not want this to be a study that would be published in one or more academic, peer-reviewed publications.

Now, we should note that all three authors have PhDs, and each of us has spent at least some time working in higher education, so we certainly have nothing against more academic research. However, our mission as leadership development consultants is to help leaders in our client organ-izations improve, and we wanted this study to be very accessible and prac-tical to the sorts of people we actually work with.

A second principle we decided on at the outset was that we wanted this study to be primarily qualitative. Our approach was to use some numeri-cal criteria for identifying our sample of leaders, and then we adopted the interview method as our primary approach to this research. More specifi-cally, we have identified a sample of leaders in several client organizations who were the most improved in our leadership development programs, and then we conducted structured, in-depth interviews with those leaders in order to answer the question: What did they do to improve so much?

We believed, and still believe, that for a qualitative (or interview-based) study such as this, doing a "deep dive" on a sample of leaders who improved significantly over the course of a six- to nine-month period would pro-vide some tremendously valuable insights. Indeed, our intention was to not only add these insights to the field of leadership development, but also to incorporate them into our own work as leadership development consul-tants. In short, this was intended from the start to be a very practical, applied study.

Of course, there are many ways to arrive at the results of a study, includ-ing using sophisticated statistical analysis (which, incidentally, we often use in our client work, especially when doing large-scale employee engage-ment surveys). And, while we acknowledge that each method has value, we believe that an interview-based approach is especially appropriate in light of the nature and purpose of this study.

With these guidelines in mind, we confronted the question: How do we identify the leaders we would like to include in the study? Frankly, that question almost answered itself.

As noted earlier, our study was based on leaders participating in lead-ership development programs in three different organizations and three different industries. The leadership development programs varied some-what in terms of the specific training, coaching, and action-learning

Figure 1.2

methods, but one thing they had in common was that they all involved two generations of 360-degree feedback, as discussed earlier.

The simplest way to come up with a sample of leaders for this study was to identify the leaders who were in the top half of all leaders in these programs in terms of perceived overall improvement. Figure 1.2 further illustrates the makeup of the sample of leaders for this study (the top half), in comparison with the leaders who were not selected for this study (the bottom half).

We readily acknowledge that there are more statistically sophisticated methods of identifying leaders who have improved significantly over time, especially if the researchers are starting with a large population of subjects (in this case, leaders). However, for a study that is intended to be a deep dive on a sample of leaders, and that is intended to be applied and practical, we believe that this method more than passes the smell test for what is reasonable when determining the leaders for this sort of study. In sum, our goal was to identify the leaders who improved the most from time one to time two, and to then ask: How did they improve?

Now, while our approach to identifying our sample of "most improved leaders" was relatively straightforward, we find it noteworthy that when we compare "top-half" and "bottom- half" leaders from our larger population of leaders, based on the other two types of questions we asked, the trends are the same. For example, as Figure 1.3 illustrates, there was a notable difference between top-half and bottom-half leaders when it came to perceptions about the extent to which leaders in our study actually worked to address areas for development that surfaced in the 360-degree feedback phase of the development effort:

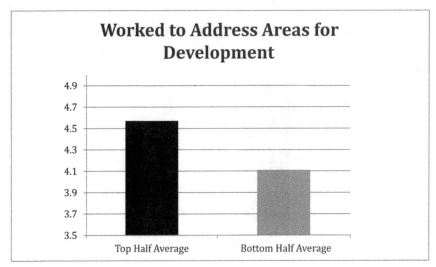

Figure 1.3

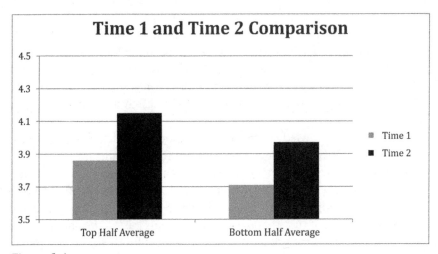

Figure 1.4

Further, there was also a notable difference between top-half and bottom-half leaders when it came to the time 1 versus time 2 scores on the four of five survey items that each leader had identified as reflecting the areas for development to work on, as illustrated in Figure 1.4.

In short, our top-half leaders (or what we refer to from this point on as our "most improved leaders") clearly outshone their bottom-half counterparts in terms of overall perceived improvement, efforts to address areas for development, and improvement in specific areas they were focusing on related to their effectiveness as leaders. Thus, there are any number of ways in which we could have identified the sample of leaders that we would include in our study, and we ended up going with the simplest—overall perceived improvement.

Having identified our sample, the next task was to determine what questions to ask. The authors of this book, who collectively have well over 50 years of experience in the field of leadership development, collaborated to come up with an interview guide with questions designed to get at what our most improved leaders actually did to get better.

We then sought and received permission from the three client organizations represented in this study to conduct interviews with our "How Leaders Improve" sample. All interviews were conducted by one of the three authors over an 18-month period. All interviewees were asked the exact same questions, although follow-up questions were used based on people's responses. Interviewers typed interviewees' responses as close to verbatim as possible.

At the end of the interview process, we had lots of interview data. Now our task was to wade through all of the interview notes in order to identify themes. In other words, we now had the raw material necessary to answer the question: How do leaders really improve? We decided that the idea of "key insights" represented a good way of structuring the remainder of this book. Finally, after having identified insights based on our data analysis, and after having supported these insights with data from our interviews, we decided that we would incorporate examples from our own experiences that validated, added color to, or even challenged our findings.

So, following this chapter, the remainder of the book (with the exception of the final chapter) will be divided into chapters representing the "key insights" that ultimately came out of our study. And now, in response to the question of how leaders improve, we enthusiastically offer the following 10 insights, each of which will be explored in detail in the chapters that follow.

1. Ripeness (from the Inside Out)
2. Ripeness (from the Outside In)
3. Central Issue
4. Penetrating Message
5. Guiding Metaphor
6. Critical Conversations
7. Training Experience
8. Social Support
9. Keep it Real (with Yourself and Others)
10. Focus on Strengths . . . and Weaknesses

CHAPTER TWO

Ripeness (from the Inside Out)

It all starts with ripeness. Years before we decided to abandon our lifelong goal of never writing a book, a couple of the authors, along with another close colleague, began having conversations about commonalities we observed among our most successful coaching engagements (that is, those engagements in which we had seen the leader make the most noteworthy and long-lasting changes). Although a number of attributes of these engagements were cited, the authors decided at that time that the biggest driver of successful coaching was the "ripeness" of the leader we were working with.

Ripeness is a term that we came up with to describe a leader's readiness to improve in general and/or in a particular area. Quite simply, we have observed that some leaders are more ripe for development than others. When a leader is ripe for a change, he or she is far more likely than average to improve, regardless of the specific nature of any feedback, training, and/or coaching the leader may receive. Put differently, as Lao Tzu is claimed to have written, "When the student is ready, the teacher will appear."[1]

Ripeness is a precursor to development. Once an individual has crossed a certain threshold level of ripeness, he or she will take actions to develop him- or herself. Prior to crossing this threshold, he or she will be actively or passively resistant to change. In these instances, development efforts will not yield improvements. Thus, coaches and other development professionals are well served to assess and address ripeness prior to engaging in development efforts. Figure 2.1 clarifies what it means for one to be ripe and also helps distinguish between ripeness and development.

If a leader is not ripe for development, then we believe one of two things should happen. One option is for the sponsor of the leadership development effort (generally, either the organization or the leader's boss) to decide not to invest in a leader's development until the leader is more ripe for the

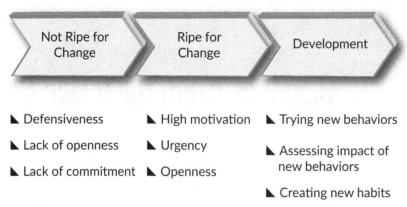

Not Ripe for Change	Ripe for Change	Development
▲ Defensiveness	▲ High motivation	▲ Trying new behaviors
▲ Lack of openness	▲ Urgency	▲ Assessing impact of new behaviors
▲ Lack of commitment	▲ Openness	▲ Creating new habits

Figure 2.1

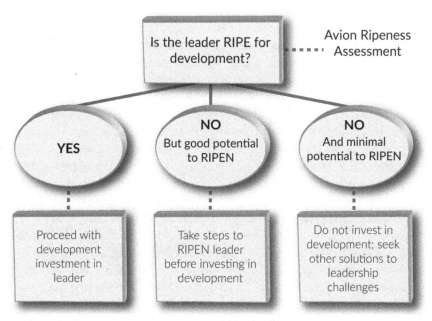

Figure 2.2

development. A second option is for a manager or skilled leadership development professional to work with the leader in order to help ripen that leader for improvement, well *before* getting into lots of specific ideas regarding how the leader could be more effective. This decision tree is highlighted in Figure 2.2.

A couple of us had the good fortune to work with Marshall Goldsmith earlier in our careers. We suspect that many readers of this book will know Goldsmith, who has been widely lauded as one of the most influential figures in the field of leadership development over the past couple of decades. On more than one occasion, one of us heard Goldsmith tell a group of leaders the story of a senior executive he was coaching who worked for a financial services client. This leader was very intelligent, successful, and driven, but was not seen as someone who always treated others with respect and dignity. Or, to put it more bluntly, he was seen by many as a jerk. Yet, in light of all this leader's success, he was not exactly ripe for the coaching.

That is, he was not ripe for the coaching until Goldsmith had the chutzpah to get the leader's spouse and other family members on the phone and the leader had to confront the reality that those closest to him perceived him similarly.

This apparently resulted in a personal epiphany for this leader, who started to look very differently at how he was living his life and the impact he was having on others. And, as the story goes, he actually did improve significantly as a leader—once he had become ripe for the improvement! As the old psychologist joke goes, "How many therapists does it take to change a light bulb? One, but the light bulb has to really want to change."

As we analyzed our interview data, we heard one example after another of factors that made our most improved leaders ripe for improvement. We actually did not use the term *ripeness* per se in our interview questions. Rather, we asked more open-ended questions that got interviewees reflecting on why they had improved so much, without steering them too far in the direction of any particular insights we had in mind.

Then we scrutinized our interview notes to see if there was evidence that our most improved leaders were particularly ready, or ripe, for improvement. And, indeed, we did find such evidence. Some of the factors contributing to a leader's ripeness were intrinsic and others extrinsic to the leader. In this chapter, we will describe the intrinsic factors that we found to be associated with a leader's ripeness for improvement, offer a model we have come up that can be used to assess a leader's ripeness, and highlight how this model can be used to help leaders become more ripe for improvement. In the next chapter, we will review the extrinsic factors we found to be associated with a leader's ripeness, and we will detail how these extrinsic factors relate to or impact the intrinsic ripeness factors highlighted in this chapter.

Issue-Specific Versus Trait Ripeness

Individuals can vary both in their general readiness to engage in self-development (trait-level ripeness), as well as their readiness to improve themselves in a specific area (issue-specific ripeness). To illustrate, Michael Jordan is one of the best basketball players of all time, and Jordan was renowned for his practice of intensely focusing on one specific element of his game to improve every off-season. One year it was improving his strength and conditioning to combat the physical style of play of Bill Lambeer and the rest of the Detroit Pistons' "Bad Boys." During another off-season, he focused on improving his free-throw shooting, and in another year, he worked on elevating his defensive game. This sort of behavior is reflective of an individual who exhibits trait-level ripeness.

Conversely, the authors have worked with leaders who are not particularly open to continuous improvement, but for some reason, evidence a ripeness to make a specific improvement in their leadership style (perhaps due to an epiphany, as illustrated by the above-referenced Marshall Goldsmith example). Both trait-level ripeness and issue-specific ripeness are valid concepts in our opinion, so we will be providing examples of each throughout the remainder of this chapter (which focuses on intrinsic ripeness) and the chapter that follows (which focuses on extrinsic ripeness).

Ripeness Mindsets

As we waded into the data collected from our most improved leaders, we noticed that they tended to adopt some consistent mindsets that seemed to predispose them to being ripe. These mindsets are summarized in Figure 2.3.

Openness

Perhaps the most prominent intrinsic factor related to ripeness that we saw in our data was simply the leader's *openness* to the entire development process. Numerous interviewees highlighted a general openness to feedback and to anything that might help them to get better in general. As one leader put it, "I was open to improving; I think generally my disposition is that I feel like I'm a work in progress and always have a bent toward this." Similarly, others noted that their motivation for participating in the leadership development program was just to get feedback, to be willing to change, and to seek to better oneself.

As another leader put it, "I have always had a hunger to improve—no matter what the area of need might be—I just always want to get better. So this process will help me know what I can work on and where to focus my improvement efforts." Based on our research, this is a great starting place for improvement.

Of course, most leaders, if asked directly, would probably claim that they are open to changing, interested in improving, and so on. So, while openness is critical, a manager, facilitator, or coach seeking to help a leader

Figure 2.3

improve needs to be skilled at looking for signs indicating *genuine* openness to a *specific* type of change. However, this attribute of openness and general motivation to improve oneself proved to be a powerful mindset associated with many of our most improved leaders.

Ambition

A second mindset we identified in our analysis that was associated with one's ripeness was the *ambition* of the leader. Some of our most improved leaders indicated that their ripeness for improvement had to do with the fact that they anticipated some opportunity to take their careers to a higher level at some point in the foreseeable future. And, to the extent that they saw the program that were participating in as a way of positioning themselves for some sort of career advancement down the road, they wanted to take full advantage of that opportunity. In other words, their ambition provided a compelling "why" for them to go through the challenge of making changes to their approach to leadership.

One leader in our sample captured the essence of this factor very nicely, stating that, "I was at a point in my career where I was committed to getting to the next level, so I welcomed this opportunity; it was a well thought-out, structured program, and I wanted to take advantage of it." In other words, even though there was no opportunity for advancement right in front of the leader, there was a level of ambition that caused that leader to want to capitalize as fully as possible on the leadership development experience that was being offered.

A variation on this theme is that a savvy manager of a high-performing leader can use a leadership development experience to be responsive to an ambitious direct report. To illustrate, one of our most improved leaders noted that her manager was perceptive enough to recognize that she was getting restless in her current position and that the manager needed to do something to demonstrate his confidence in her and his willingness to invest in her, even though there was not a specific, more senior position that she could plausibly move into within the organization at that time. As she put it, "my manger knew what I needed to be motivated, and knew this would keep me in my seat a bit longer." In other words, she was ambitious, and her manager recognized that, and—given realistic organizational constraints—used the leadership development program as a way of acknowledging and supporting her ambition while also seeking out additional opportunities for his direct report.

At the same time, some of our most improved leaders indicated that they believed that making progress on their development goals would position them well for a *specific* future job opportunity (e.g., replacing their boss). We refer to this in the next chapter, since we believe that the potential for advancement into a specific role is an extrinsic factor that capitalizes on one's inherent ambition.

To summarize this ripeness mindset, our most improved leaders tended to be ambitious people, and a number of them saw the leadership development experience they were being offered as a way of helping to position themselves for a career move down the road. As one of our most improved leaders put it, "You never know when a promotion may come along, so you need to always be focused on self-improvement."

Desire for ROI

At the outset of some of our leadership development programs, we note to the group that an investment is being made for them to be there, and then we ask: Exactly what is being invested? Almost invariably, we hear two responses: "Money and time" (and "time," of course, *is* "money"). Our next question, typically, is: If an investment is being made, what would you then hope for or expect? The answer, of course, is "a return on investment," or ROI.

The notion that any sound investment should lead to an ROI allows us to talk about the valuable time of the participants themselves. Any leadership development professional who has been in our field for any time to speak of will have undoubtedly encountered the "hostage" at some point. This is the leadership development participant who clearly "doesn't want to be there" and offers up the minimal level of engagement necessary to get through the program and check the proverbial training box.

The absence of such hostages among our most improved leaders was notable. Now, we are not saying that there were no skeptics in our sample. Rather, what we noticed was that our most improved leaders consistently demonstrated the mindset that they were determined to get value out of the leadership development experience. In other words, they expected an ROI, and actually held themselves accountable for ensuring that they got one.

This ripeness mindset turned up in a couple of ways in the interviews. First, it was noted that to participate in a leadership development program without the intention to take full advantage of it is nonsensical. One of our leaders effectively captured this idea, saying, "If you are going to put all that time and effort into it, and if you then don't make changes, it's a big waste of time." Another echoed this idea, stating, "If you don't make any changes, why did you sign up for this in the first place?"

Now, granted, not everyone in these sorts of programs actually "signs up" for the experience; some people are informed by their managers or their Human Resources department about the "good news" that they have been nominated for a leadership development program. The logic, however, remains the same: If one is going to be investing time and energy in such an experience, it only makes sense to come into it determined to ensure that there is some positive effect from the experience—in other words, some sort of ROI.

Believing That It's Important

Another finding from our research highlights a common mindset of individuals who are ripe for improvement. One of our interview questions was as follows: "On a scale of 1–10, how important did you think it was to make changes based on any / all of this [360-degree] feedback?" The average rating in response to that question was a 9.3. And by far the most common response to that question was a 10.

When asked to provide a rationale for one's rating, the responses highlighted two clear themes. First, as referenced above, these individuals demonstrated a commitment to self-improvement.

Second, a number of our leaders identified likely incentives that rendered improvement in an area particularly important to them. As one leader indicated, "I knew I probably would not get to a higher level without improving in the key area that surfaced in my feedback." For this individual, "getting to a higher level" was an important incentive. Similarly, another leader noted that, "If I had not gotten and then addressed my feedback through this program, it could have de-railed my career." For this leader, adverse career consequences represented a negative incentive that drove the importance of making progress on the feedback. Thus, for a variety of reasons, virtually all of our most improved leaders thought that it was extremely important to take action on the feedback they had received to ensure that they were improving as leaders.

Fear of Consequences of Inaction

Some of the ripeness mindsets we've highlighted above can be considered rewards, or "approach motivators." That is, by successfully investing effort in one's own professional development, one is *approaching* some personally meaningful value (for example, ambition, self-development, ROI, etc.). However, some of our most improved leaders also reported "avoidance motivators" as being powerful determinants of one's ripeness.

For example, one of our most improved leaders received generally excellent baseline feedback. However, this leader did have one consistently critical "outlier" in her 360-degree feedback report, someone who rated her much lower than others on a number of dimensions. The leader had just gotten a new boss, and she was concerned that this outlier would create negative perceptions with her new boss. So she decided to directly address the feedback with her new boss. As she explained it, "We had gone through a transition of executive leadership, and I wanted to put my best foot forward and make a good first impression. It was worrisome to me to have my new boss see me in that light, so I openly discussed this feedback with him right away by saying, 'I don't know if you've seen my 360 but I would like to chat with you right away.'"

In other words, this leader was motivated to avoid negative consequences, which illustrates the idea that sometimes individuals are ripe to make a change because of fear of inaction or some potential negative consequence. In short, there are numerous "ripeness mindsets" that our research indicates are clearly associated with improvement, and these mindsets are based on both approach and avoidance motivators.

Soul-Searching

Some of our most improved leaders were actually in a much different place in terms of their careers and their ambitions. As we listened to these leaders explaining why they threw themselves into the leadership development experience, we latched onto a term that one leader used to describe where she was, psychologically, emotionally, and maybe even spiritually, at the time of the leadership development experience: The term *soul-searching*.

A number of our most improved leaders seem to have been in such a place in the midst of their leadership development efforts, and they used amazingly consistent language in describing where they were at in their career journeys. For example, one leader said, "I was going through some soul-searching about my career, and that made me open to the feedback." Another leader said, "I was asking myself—should I consider leaving, or should I focus on building my career here? That caused me to take this program seriously." In short, there is some evidence that leaders who were asking bigger questions about their work lives (for example, about whether they were in the right jobs, companies, or even fields) may have been particularly ripe for improvement as leaders.

We suspect that at least some leadership development professionals can think of one or more examples of leaders they have worked with who were in a similar place, but who responded quite differently—choosing not to fully engage in a leadership development opportunity precisely because they were not sure they were even going to be around much longer. Thus, soul-searching does not guarantee ripeness. However, those who are ripe for change often appear to be going through a period of soul-searching that enables them to see things in a new light.

There are at least two lessons here. First, the leader who is going through a period of soul-searching should be open to the idea that it represents the ideal time to invest in his or her growth and development as a leader. Soul-searching, by its very nature, involves rethinking assumptions, actions, and decisions—and what better frame of mind to be in so that you can be open to feedback, counsel, new models, and new skills? Second, the manager of a leader who may be going through a period of soul-searching may find that it is the very best time to invest in that leader's growth and development. Of course, being able to do this requires that the manager of the soul-searcher be perceptive enough to be aware that his or her direct report is in the midst of such a period (which hopefully is food for thought for managers of leaders who are seeking to improve).

Commitment to Self-Improvement

Great leaders tend to see leadership as a journey more than a destination; they view themselves as a work in progress and have a commitment to self-improvement that shows up any time they have an opportunity to learn something new about leadership, and about themselves as leaders. And this quality was prominent among our most improved leaders.

Perhaps more so than any of the other mindsets related to ripeness, our most improved leaders used language to describe this mindset that made clear that intrinsic motivation to improve is a key to development as a leader. To illustrate, one leader said, "Wanting to learn and improve is key; self-motivation is the most important thing." Another echoed that idea, saying, "Improvement has got to be self-initiated. If someone isn't 100% dedicated to improving, they are not going to improve."

Commitment to self-improvement is distinct from openness in that it represents an orientation to take action on or address feedback, whereas openness is simply being receptive to the message. In other words, commitment to self-improvement implies an agency and accountability that openness does not. As one leader put it, "I was passionate about continued development as a leader," and as another said, "Any time there is a negative surprise on a feedback report, I see it as something I should address."

The age-old question is: How much of this commitment to self-improvement is the product of one's innate personality and how much can be fostered through inspiration and/or coaching from others? After all, we have all heard the question, "Are great leaders born or made?" Our answer to that question is generally, "Yes." In other words, we firmly believe that, while there are certain innate qualities that may make one predisposed to be a great leader, there are also clearly things that leaders can learn over time in order to maximize their effectiveness as leaders.

The RIPEN Model

In light of the tremendous importance of a leader's ripeness for improvement, Avion Consulting has developed a model that identifies, in a very simple and practical way, the core intrinsic dimensions of one's ripeness to improve as a leader. It is important to emphasize that we did not start out with the goal of creating a ripeness model and then look for evidence to support it in our data. Rather, we carefully analyzed the data from our study and, coupled with our understanding of the science of behavior change, identified what we believe to be the most critical ripeness levers. These levers are captured by the acronym RIPEN, and the model shown in Figure 2.4 expands our discussion of the ripeness mindsets identified above by addressing what we believe are the underlying factors the above mindsets are impacting.

The first letter in the RIPEN acronym represents "Realization," which refers to a leader having a rational awareness about and understanding of the need for a change. This realization may come in the form of an insightful "aha" that a leader gets from 360-degree feedback, from a discussion with his or her manager or coach, or from any number of other sources. However, the realization may also come in the form of feedback that reminds the leader of an already-felt need to make a change. This form of realization is more of a reinforcement or reminder rather than an "aha." One way or another, though, some of our most improved leaders learned things about themselves as a result of the leadership development process that dramatically changed their perspective on the effectiveness of their current approach.

A precursor to being ripe for making a change is having personally compelling awareness that the change needs to happen. Simply hearing a piece of feedback does not make it personally compelling. We have all heard feedback that we didn't agree with or didn't believe warranted a change.

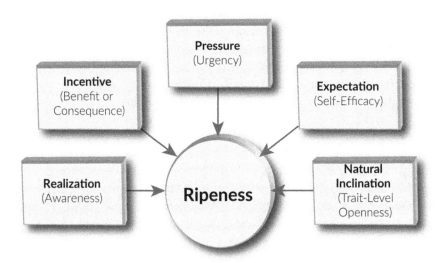

Figure 2.4

One must actively and personally identify with the need for a change and assume some level of personal accountability for the fact that one's behavior, not the external environment, is causing some suboptimal results. While it is not necessarily critical for all five core RIPEN conditions to be met in order for someone to be ripe for a change (Natural Inclination, for example, can be low even in individuals who are ripe for change), at a minimum one must have an insight about what to change and a sense of personal accountability to make meaningful progress on some specific issue.

The second letter in the RIPEN acronym represents "Incentive," meaning that the leader perceives some potential benefit to making the change, or some consequence to not making the change. Incentive is distinct from Realization in that it is not a logical understanding of the need to make a change, but rather a personally compelling motivation to make a change.

Many incentives are external in nature, such as money, promotions, and public acclaim. However, as we will highlight in the next chapter, we believe the general factor of Incentive is internal in nature, because it reflects specific outcomes the individual values or wants to avoid. In other words, money, promotions, and public acclaim are powerful incentives only if the individual values these outcomes. A powerful Incentive is one that represents a personally meaningful outcome to an individual.

Two of the most commonly cited incentives we heard from our most improved leaders were ambition and fear. Many of our most improved leaders, for instance, indicated that if they were successful in their self-development, they would be candidates for advancement, and that was a compelling motivation. Additionally, some of our most improved leaders noted that they were motivated by fear of consequences of inaction (for example, decreased influence, less job security, or not maximizing compensation).

Positive incentives (such as advancement opportunities) were much more commonly cited by our most improved leaders than were negative incentives (such as fear of being fired). This may primarily be due to the fact that most of the leaders in our sample were participants in high-potential leader development programs (and therefore were not likely to be getting "change or else" messages). Future research with less homogeneous samples should explore whether dramatic changes in effectiveness are more likely to have been motivated by approach or avoidance incentives.

Personally meaningful incentives can take various forms beyond the two examples noted above. Regardless of the specific incentive, our research suggests that skilled coaches or managers should help the leaders they are working with to identify or generate a "compelling why" that represents a personally relevant incentive for making a change prior to focusing on skill development. And, of course, the idea is to explore a leader's incentives, rather than to state what his or her incentive should be. Telling someone he or she will be promoted, for instance, may not really be an incentive to an individual who values work–life balance more than monetary rewards or public recognition.

To illustrate all of this, one of us provided 360-degree feedback to a leader who was perceived to have challenges in listening to and incorporating others' points of view. This leader was perceived to be truly open only to the ideas he and his team generated. As we transitioned from debriefing the feedback themes to generating an action plan, the individual indicated that he was a devout Christian and that his feedback suggested to him that he was not living his Christian values as well as he would have liked. No one in the feedback process cited that this leader was not behaving like a good Christian. However, both the coach and the leader realized, without using the term *ripeness,* per se, that linking the feedback to this personally meaningful values-based incentive served to ripen the leader to make some changes that others were requesting of him.

When assessing motivations or incentives, we have found that it is also important to understand what an individual's "countermotivations" are. Countermotivations are those motivators that encourage someone to continue to maintain the status quo. Fear of change, risk of failure, and complacency are examples of common countermotivations.

For example, a leader one of us has worked with was promoted to be the General Manager of a mid-sized multinational business. The leader received feedback that he wasn't using his time well. Specifically, he was involving himself too deeply in decisions, which caused him to be a bottleneck in the decision-making process, thereby demotivating his team and resulting in deadlines being missed. This individual was highly ambitious, and he hoped to translate success in his current role to becoming the CEO of a larger organization. And he did understand that he wasn't leveraging others as well as he could be.

However, he also had a strong countermotivation to prove to others that he was capable and in charge. Thus, in those critical moments when he needed to step back and empower others, this countermotivation tended to outweigh his ambition and desire to motivate his staff. Over the course of the coaching relationship, the leader was encouraged to wrestle with the question of what was more important: The need to be in control, or the desire to lead in a more scalable manner? By tapping into his internally important incentives (ambition, advancement, and being a good leader), the leader was able to overcome the countermotivations that explained his behavior and make meaningful improvements that resulted in better decision-making and higher levels of staff engagement.

The next letter in the RIPEN acronym represents "Pressure," meaning that the leader perceives some urgency to making the changes in question. Pressure is associated with making specific changes in the near term, rather than being mired in complacency or procrastination. Our most improved leaders referenced new managers, organizational changes, and opportunities to interact with C-Suite executives to whom they did not have regular exposure as meaningful forms of pressure for them.

The question a manager or a coach needs to ask in order to assess Pressure is, "Why can't making this change wait until tomorrow?" If the leader doesn't have a compelling answer to this, he or she may not be particularly ripe to make the change, despite having Realization and Incentive.

The literature in the areas of behavior change indicates that many individuals may know that a change is needed and may be personally motivated to make the change, but may have no immediate pressure or urgency to do so. In their seminal Stages of Change model, the noted alcoholism researchers Prochaska and DiClemente refer to this type of situation as someone being in either the Contemplation or the Preparation stage of change. Individuals in these stages of change cognitively understand the need to make a change and are motivated to make the change, but don't yet have an urgency driver that is propelling them to take immediate action.[2]

The fourth letter in the RIPEN acronym represents "Expectation," which refers to an individual's expectation that he or she will successfully make the change in question (in other words, a leader's self-efficacy to make the change). Albert Bandura defines self-efficacy as one's belief in one's ability to succeed in specific situations or to accomplish a specific task.[3] Self-efficacy plays a major role in how one approaches goals, tasks, and challenges. Quite simply, leaders who are more confident in their ability to make a change are riper than those who are less confident in their ability.

Factors that impact one's Expectation include one's level of success in making prior changes, as well as a well-thought-out plan for addressing the specific development goal. However, there are also a number of extrinsic factors that directly impact Expectation (role models, supportive bosses, involvement in relevant training, provision of a coach, etc.). These extrinsic factors will be reviewed in more detail in the next chapter. The bottom line is that ripe leaders have a high level of confidence in their ability to make a change, which enables them to overcome the inevitable setbacks they are likely to face in making any significant change in their approach to leadership.

The fifth and final letter in the RIPEN acronym represents "Natural Inclination," or one's trait-level openness to change. Our most improved leaders frequently referenced commitment to self-improvement or openness to changing in general as drivers of their behavior changes, and these are reflective of our dimension of Natural Inclination. In her bestselling book Mindset, Stanford social psychologist Carol Dweck asserts that individuals hold one of two very powerful mindsets that unconsciously shape their behaviors and actions.[4]

The majority of individuals naturally appear to possess what she refers to as a "fixed mindset." This refers to a self-perception that our intelligence or talents are more or less fixed traits. People with this mindset approach their life and work in a way that proves that their natural talent is the greatest determinant of their success or failure. Individuals with a fixed mindset are generally less open to leadership development efforts and could be thought of as being less committed to self-improvement, on the basis of having a mindset that suggests that they aren't likely to change much.

Conversely, Dweck found that a smaller subset of people naturally possess what she refers to as a "growth mindset." These individuals believe that their most basic abilities can be developed through curiosity, dedication, and hard work. In other words, while natural talent matters to these individuals, they believe it is just a starting point. These individuals are intrinsically more "open" when presented with leadership development opportunities, thereby exhibiting one of the traits of ripeness. This trait level openness is one of the powerful determinants of one's ripeness.

As mentioned previously, it is necessary for an individual to have a specific Realization in order to be ripe (in other words, it's actually a *requirement* in order for one to be ripe). For the other four factors, however, the more of the RIPEN dimensions that are "high" or activated for a particular change, the more ripe the individual is for a particular change. For example, if someone has had a significant Realization and displays high levels of Natural Inclination, but lacks Incentive, Pressure, and/or Expectation, he or she is less likely to make a change than someone who is high across all five dimensions for a particular change.

We would like to highlight the role ripeness plays in a coaching engagement by exploring the case of one particularly ripe leader we coached. This leader's central issue (this theme will be explored in detail in Chapter 4) was that she appeared to be too nice with employees in situations that probably called for difficult conversations or remedial action. The leader had received feedback from a variety of senior stakeholders that she was far too permissive of underperformance and appeared to be too protective of her team members. This protectiveness inhibited the team's ability to make the strategic changes that were required of the department. She had been told that if she were not able to make changes in this aspect of her leadership style, she might be demoted or even fired.

Her Realization was that, in an effort to be caring, she was not holding others to the same levels of performance to which she held herself. Furthermore, if she were to lose her job, her successor would likely hold others accountable with less care and consideration than she would. Therefore, she concluded that holding others more accountable actually *would,* in effect, be demonstrating care for others.

The leader also had plenty of Incentive to change. The immediate incentive was negative, or avoidance-oriented, in nature. If she did not make meaningful progress in her key development area, it was at least somewhat likely that meaningful, negative, external consequences (for example, losing her job) could result. The economic consequences of this possibility alone represented a powerful avoidance motivator to the leader.

Early on during the course of the coaching engagement, the leader also came to the insight that holding others accountable to high standards was in line with her values of care and achievement. She realized that she could demonstrate more care for others and achieve even greater results if she evolved her leadership so that she was more demanding and candid with her direct reports. This incentive (enhanced team performance) became her aspirational approach motivator.

With respect to the next element of our RIPEN model, Pressure—the six-month-long coaching engagement had been initiated because her boss expected the leader to make meaningful improvements. The leader knew that making these changes could not wait; she needed to address the performance concerns immediately. In fact, the day after debriefing her feedback, she called her leadership coach to explore exactly how to approach a specific difficult discussion. This proactivity suggested to her coach that the leader did not think she could or should wait to implement the changes. The leader did indeed feel Pressure as a result of her boss's perceptions that she needed to quickly make the desired changes.

Expectation, as explained earlier, relates to the leader's self-confidence to make the change. Interestingly, 15 years earlier the leader had received 360-degree feedback indicating that she was *too* direct and demanding of her subordinates. The leader concluded that she must have swung the pendulum too far toward being a collaborative and inspirational leader, at the expense of results. The leader was very confident that she could be more direct but was significantly less confident in her ability to balance a results orientation with a relationship orientation. Thus, the confidence-building needed to occur around simultaneously living these values (a very difficult proposition for many leaders we've worked with).

The leader and her coach identified organizational role models whom she believed exhibited this balance effectively. Additionally, the leader used the coach as a sounding board to explore tailored options for holding specific individuals accountable. Finally, the coach recommended some good readings and videos on the topic to advance the leader's knowledge of how to balance these potentially competing values. Eventually, the leader generated a reasonably high level of confidence that she could balance the seemingly competing priorities of results and relationships. This confidence was later reinforced when her boss commented to her that he was seeing her make noteworthy changes and also when some of her direct reports indicated that they appreciated her enhanced clarity and directness with the team.

Finally, the leader exhibited a fairly high level of Natural Inclination to pursue self-development. As indicated above, the leader had previously received feedback and made noteworthy improvements to her leadership by enhancing her inspiration and collaboration tendencies. However, there were other instances in which the leader had not successfully acted on feedback, so it would not be accurate to say the individual had exceptionally high Natural Inclination.

Nonetheless, over the course of the coaching engagement, the leader made very meaningful changes in her behavior. Her boss noticed these behaviors, and her team was actually more motivated by her new approach to leadership. In fact, her boss gave her the highest performance rating possible on the year-end review and actually positioned her to advance into a more senior role the next year. These changes were largely driven by the leader's initial ripeness to make some changes, which was contributed to by her boss, her coach, her team, and her own natural tendencies.

This case study illustrates the nature and importance of each of the five key elements of a leader's intrinsic ripeness to improve: Realization, Incentive, Pressure, Expectation, and Natural Inclination. And, as noted earlier in this chapter, each of these aspects of intrinsic ripeness surfaced in our research. In addition to the intrinsic ripeness factors discussed in this chapter, our most improved leaders also referenced a number of extrinsic factors that impacted their ripeness. These factors will be discussed in the next chapter, and the relationship between intrinsic and extrinsic factors will be explored.

Recommendations

For the Leader

- Assess yourself using the RIPEN model. If you are low on one or more elements of intrinsic ripeness, reflect on the implications of this. Consider discussing with a boss, coach, or other trusted stakeholder.

- Link feedback and developmental objectives to personal values in order to ensure stronger commitment to behavioral commitments.
- Internalize the need for change by considering which of the seven ripeness mindsets resonate for you as a reason for making a significant change. Those who intend to make changes simply because others raise an area in a review or a 360-degree feedback report are far less likely to make long-term, meaningful improvement.
- Identify compelling motivators (for example, promotion or alignment with values) or the risks to not making the changes (for example, decreased internal influence or potential risk of termination).

For the Organization

- Utilize the RIPEN model or the associated assessment (which can be accessed at www.howleadersimprove.com) to determine if someone is likely to make a specific change.
- After reviewing an individual's RIPEN assessment results, consider what the organization or supervisor should do to further ripen the leader for a specific change in order to make the change more likely.
- When enlisting leaders for participation in a leadership development initiative, speak with them and their managers to ensure that they have sufficient bandwidth to properly focus on the experience. If not, consider restructuring priorities to ensure that they do have sufficient bandwidth.
- Encouraging semi-public sharing of action plans is a commitment that creates an urgency driver. At the very least, action plans should be shared with one's manager.
- Invest in and provide tangible support (training, internal partner, external coach, etc.) to those who are ripe.

For the Coach

- Listen carefully for indications of ripeness. Most leaders will likely say they are "open," but analyzing a leader's other comments and actions to have a better understanding of their true ripeness is critical.
- Have the leader you are working with consider which of the seven ripeness mindsets resonate with him or her as a reason to make the change.
- When reflecting on feedback that causes the leader you are working with to feel defensive, ask him or her what he or she is doing to contribute to the outcome. In other words, try to get him or her internalize rather than externalize the source of the problem.

- Explicitly explore and address countermotivations that can inhibit the leader you are working with from making changes.
- Utilize the RIPEN model to structure coaching conversations. Coaching should explore the five elements of the framework and focus on those elements in which an individual is relatively low, as this is what will likely inhibit a leader from making meaningful progress on his or her development goals.
- Find the incentives that will help someone become more ripe, such as career upside, internal motivations like tenacity, and even negative outcomes for a leader and/or his or her direct reports if the leader fails to change.

Can a leader be
" too ripe?"

unfocused goals,
lack of esteem,
people-pleaser-
overwhelmed

CHAPTER THREE

Ripeness (from the Outside In)

In the previous chapter, we highlighted the *intrinsic* factors that contribute to an individual's ripeness for change (Realization, Incentive, Pressure, Expectation and Natural Inclination). However, through our research we found that our most improved leaders also consistently cited a number of *extrinsic* factors that significantly impacted their ripeness for change. Just as sunlight enables fruit to ripen, so do external factors contribute to the ripeness of leaders to engage in a sincere effort to improve themselves. We will explore those factors in this chapter.

Before proceeding, however, let us delve into another short case study to illustrate the concept. We recently worked with the regional head of Asia for a large, global financial services provider. In this capacity, she was seen as a natural leader—someone who excelled at both representing the business externally and leading courageously within the organization. However, her reputation had been a bit tarnished because of frequently voiced concerns about her ability to effectively manage the execution of the projects she led. Specifically, in an interview-based 360-degree review process, individuals reported that she was much more effective at initiating projects (rallying initial support both up and down the organization) than she was at ensuring excellent execution. This led to senior leaders in the organization having reservations about her ability to assume positions of greater responsibility.

However, a critical senior leader suddenly departed the organization, and this created a cascading series of open roles to fill in the organization. The leader's immediate manager advocated on her behalf, arguing that she would be a good fit for a position of increased scale and responsibility in the organization's New York headquarters. The executive team decided to bring the leader back to New York and give her a chance to prove herself in this expanded role. In fact, it was insinuated to the leader that if she could execute flawlessly and effectively manage the projects under her scope of responsibility, she could be in line for a position of even greater responsibility. The leader's new boss was very supportive of her and, in fact, also encouraged her to continue leveraging her executive coach (one of the authors). The leader was particularly motivated by the potential future promotion, as it would be into a role in which she had long been very interested.

Over the ensuing year, she did in fact prove to be quite successful in flawlessly executing the responsibilities in her new position. In fact, she was perceived as having made significant improvements in her leadership style and was ultimately promoted again, heading a global business unit. This true story illustrates several extrinsic factors related to one's ripeness that we heard consistently from our most improved leaders. Specifically, we identified four such factors through our research, and each will be addressed in turn.

Potential for Advancement

Perhaps the most widely cited external factor contributing to ripeness among our most improved leaders was potential for advancement. When a leader knows that he or she is being looked at for a higher-level position and knows that demonstrated improvement in one or more areas will make promotion more likely, that tends to result in ripeness for growth and development. This certainly was true in the case of the leader we discussed above who moved from Asia to New York, and we also consistently heard the same thing from many of our most improved leaders. Let us cite a couple of examples.

One of our most improved leaders was a Regional Sales Manager overseeing a large region of retail stores. His manager was planning to retire within the next year or two, and this leader knew that he was at least a candidate to succeed his boss. This leader was already seen as being a very strong leader, but some areas for development were identified in his 360-degree feedback. Since he had come from another industry (though still in retail), and since he knew he would be competing with some home-grown talent for the senior job, he was highly motivated to demonstrate that his outside experience would be an asset and at the same time that he understood the company's industry and culture well enough to be in the most senior position in his function within the company.

In other words, for this individual, the extrinsic factor of an advancement opportunity represented a meaningful incentive, which in turn enhanced his ripeness for change (see Figure 3.1). For individuals who were less ambitious or did not value the incentives a potential promotion represented, a potential advancement opportunity would not have represented an external ripening factor.

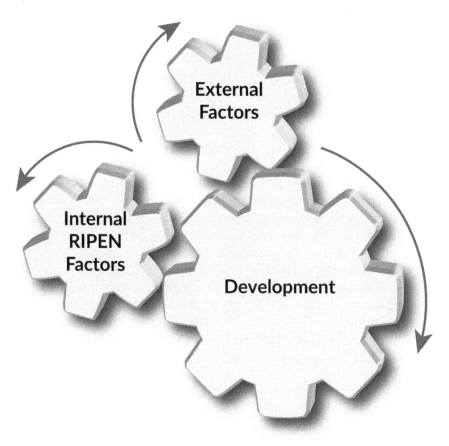

Figure 3.1

Another of our most improved leaders was in a similar situation, as the number two person in the finance organization of her company and someone who was at least a plausible candidate for the number one position when it opens up. While her manager was not on the verge of retirement, he was clearly much closer to retirement than she was. This leader was extremely strong technically and unanimously perceived as having impeccable integrity. Her challenge was that her very quiet, humble, understated approach to leadership caused others to wonder whether she would be a good fit for a senior executive position. While humble, however, she also acknowledged that she thought she had the competence and character for the top job and that she relished the challenge inherent in stretching herself in pursuit of a C-level position.

In other words, she was ripe for the leadership development opportunity because of external factors that were relevant to what she intrinsically found motivating. As with the first example above, she did improve significantly—and, as of this writing, she is being groomed as the internal successor to the Chief Financial Officer when he retires.

These are just two cases, but they are illustrative of a common theme from our interviews: When a more senior manager tells a given leader that he or she is being considered for a specific, more senior role, it tends to enhance that leader's ripeness for improvement. And, in general, we are not talking about advancement at some vague point in the future; we are talking about being promoted into a particular role at a particular point in time, as was the case with each of the two leaders in the examples cited above.

Most often, the specific role was that of the direct supervisor of the leader with whom we were working. And most often, that leader was hoping to advance following the pending retirement of his or her boss. Consistent with these examples, sometimes leaders ended up being in one of our high-potential leadership development programs specifically as a part of the organization's succession planning efforts. In other cases, the advancement opportunity was less clearly defined (with a leader simply being told she was "ready for the next step," for example). But the key with this factor was that certain leaders were riper for development when they connected the development experience they were participating in to an advancement opportunity.

This ripeness, based on the opportunity at hand, manifested itself in a number of ways: When invited to participate in the leadership development program, these leaders agreed; they showed up to the group and one-on-one coaching sessions; they completed all the work that they were expected to complete as a part of the program (for example, developing an action plan, writing a business case for a project that was part of the program, etc.). Put simply, they had an incentive to take the program seriously and to make clear that they were doing so to those who had sponsored their participation in the program. And, it should be noted, the programs in which they were participating were specifically designed to help leaders develop in ways that would make them stronger candidates for the higher-level positions for which they were being considered.

Although a number of our most improved leaders were being considered as candidates for specific, more senior roles in the not-too-distant future, other leaders viewed this as a potential benefit in the future, but didn't have a clear line of sight as to the precise nature of the potential promotion opportunity. As one leader indicated:

> "I wasn't thinking that I was up for promotion, although there was a position open above me. Nor was I seen as a potential successor. But, I was looking at this for the next time around. I thought, 'Time's running out,

and the next time this comes up, I'm going to be ready.' I also thought, 'Maybe I would have been a successor this time if I were stronger in terms of my key area for development,' which is leadership presence. I am now a lot more confident that I'll be considered for the most senior role next time, although I know I still have areas to work on."

This leader had the self-awareness to realize that he was not a plausible candidate for the most senior position in his function at the time he was in his high-potential leadership development program, but he firmly believed that the program offered him an opportunity to work on some leadership skills that would make him a viable candidate the *next* time around. That is the sort of thing that our most improved leaders do!

Transition

For some of our most improved leaders, another contextual factor they reported as enhancing their ripeness for personal growth was not merely the *prospect* of moving into another role; it was the *actuality* of being in the midst of a transition. In addition to the example cited at the beginning of this chapter, a few more examples from our most improved leaders illustrate this factor.

One of our leaders had just moved into the role of President of one business unit within her organization, and she said her mindset as the leadership development program kicked off was, "Wow, if I'm going to take on more responsibility, I should be getting better as a leader." She further noted that the things she ended up working on over the course of the program, such as being more strategic, were very important in light of her new role and responsibilities. Thus, her motivation to grow in these areas was enhanced by her role transition. It seems that in this leader's case, the internal ripeness factor that was most activated by being in a transition was Realization (the insight that she did not have all the skills she needed to be successful in her new role).

Another of our most improved leaders was in the midst of a different sort of transition. As she explained it, "I think what really helped me is I was in transition between jobs; I had come out of one job and was moving back into an area I was familiar with." This leader went on to explain that having just made that move gave her time to focus her efforts, absorb her feedback, and focus on her unique action items. She added, "I don't think I would have been as successful if I had been doing this while in my previous position."

In this case, the recent transition back into a familiar area of responsibility and reporting to a leader with whom she was comfortable enhanced the leader's ripeness by providing her with the time and focus she needed to make headway on long-standing development areas. Thus, in her case the internal ripeness factors that appear to have been most activated were Realization (giving her time to absorb the feedback) and Expectation (in the sense that reporting to a familiar boss gave her the confidence to take risks in evolving her leadership approach).

One final example illustrates how being in the midst of a transition can result in a leader being riper for development. One of our most improved leaders was on maternity leave when she got the invitation to participate in her organization's high-potential leadership development program, and she said that she was "excited to come back to work." She indicated that the freshness and challenge of the role caused her to have a new perspective on her growth and development that motivated her performance. Again, it appears that being in the midst of a transition caused the individual to soul-search and have big-picture realizations about her need to develop professionally.

These examples illustrate three different ways in which being in the midst of a transition is an external factor that promotes ripeness and improvement: An immediate need to grow in a given area; an ability to focus on development more than might typically be the case; and a heightened level of excitement about moving from one type of situation (such as being on leave) to another (such as rejoining one's team). In each of these examples, being in the midst of a transition impacted the internal RIPEN factor of Realization. We believe this was the result of the transitions providing the leaders with fresh challenges and perspectives that caused them to have new insights about their need to develop.

There is one final point we'd like to make related to the transition factor. A question we as leadership consultants sometimes get is whether we think it makes sense for a leader to participate in a leadership development program when the leader is in the midst of a transition. While every situation is different, our general response is: Yes, we think it's a great time to do it. In fact, we often counsel leaders we work with who are in such transitions that the feedback and follow-up processes that are part of our programs represent a great way of essentially introducing oneself to one's new team and of getting off to a strong start.

In our experience, when a leader in transition tells his or her new team, "I have gotten some feedback as part of a leadership development program I'm participating in, and here are some of my strengths and areas for development" it helps to establish a team climate of openness, humility, and self-development—all positive things for a team in transition. Additionally, it appears that being in transition is an external factor that can enable leaders to adopt a more open and flexible mindset toward their own development, provided they are approaching the change with sufficiently positive mindsets (confidence, security, engagement, etc.).

Organizational Change

We think it's a pretty safe assumption that anybody reading this book either has been, is, or will be involved in some sort of a major organizational change. In fact, just over the course of this study (a period of about two years from the date when we first started gathering data to the moment this chapter is being written), the organizations in our study have gone through the following changes: A large acquisition, the hiring of a new President and CEO, a change to an entirely new operating model, a major systems implementation, and an enormous shift in legislation directly and significantly impacting one organization's industry. And these are just the changes that come immediately to mind; there are no doubt many other changes, both large and small, that employees within these organizations have experienced over the past couple of years.

Interestingly, sometimes our clients tell us that they want to hold off on development initiatives, such as high-potential leadership development programs, until they have gotten through some sort of a major change. Again, every situation is different, and we acknowledge that there are probably cases in which this makes sense. However, in general we don't subscribe to this point of view, for at least two reasons.

First, as many people reading this book can likely attest, change in the organizational world these days is a constant. And second, based on our research, possibly the *best* time for a leader to participate in a development experience is when he or she is involved in some sort of significant organizational change (as these changes "bait the hook" for leaders to grow and improve themselves).

There are a couple examples from our research that illustrate this idea very vividly. The first one has to do with an organization that was in the early stages of a shift to a new operating model as a group of leaders began one of the annual high-potential leadership development programs that our firm runs for this organization. This change impacted (and, in fact, is still impacting) literally every area within the company, and many leaders throughout the organization have different types of leadership responsibility for aligning their areas with the new model.

One such leader was in the leadership development program that was just starting up, and this leader ended up being one of our most improved leaders at the end of the six-month program. When interviewed about reasons for her significant improvement, she cited "the amount of change we are going through as an organization and the implications for me," adding that she thought it was a "good time to expand my skill set."

Some of the challenges faced by leaders going through this change included things like being able to articulate the case for the change effectively, leading teams through various specific changes related to the larger transition, effectively managing the conflict that is inherent in any large-scale change effort, and so on. And the leadership development program in which the leader in this example participated included modules on each of these critical leadership skills. So, we wholeheartedly agree with the assessment of this particular leader when she says that the fact that her organization was going through a major change made it a particularly good time for her, as one of the leaders of the change effort, to be working on her leadership skills. In considering which of the RIPEN factors organizational change appears to have been activated for this leader, we believe that both Realization (insight about the need to change) and Pressure (urgency to make the change in the near future) are likely suspects.

A second example comes from another of our most improved leaders—this one a leader in Information Technology. As this leader explained, "We were going through a very focused type of change, and it involved my whole team of 70—and they were saying, 'this is not working.'" This, of course, is not an unusual scenario. Studies over the past 20 years or so have consistently found that organizational change efforts frequently fail to achieve their intended results. The consulting firm Towers Watson conducted one of the more recent of these studies. Their conclusion: "Less than half of respondents across a variety of industries around the world indicate they achieved the desired operational goals from change initiatives."[1]

Fortunately for this leader, the 360-degree feedback she received as a part of her leadership development program included some specific feedback on what was not working with regard to her change leadership, and what some options might be for addressing the issues that others were concerned about. And at the end of the six-month program, some of the feedback she got was that the increased success that her organization was experiencing with the change effort was due in part to her having "matured as a leader a great deal" over the course of the program. Thus, once again, the organizational change likely enhanced this leader's ripeness to grow and develop and resulted in her being one of our most improved leaders. Again, it strikes us that organizational change activated the internal ripeness factors of Realization and Pressure for this individual.

Yet another example underscores how leadership development programs can help both in developing the leader and also in developing followers at every level. For one leader, it became evident that the pace of change required that this individual truly "step up" as a leader, particularly given the fact that the organizational environment was not ideal during the change. So, her development as a leader meant she could be a buffer for her team during these volatile changes. As the leader explained, "I knew I had to figure out how to train myself, and also figure out how to train and bring employees on board—while running a business that was working well but didn't have enough resources." This change inspired the leader to become accountable during a period of time that was especially challenging, both for the leader and for her employees.

So, when pressed on the question of whether or not it makes sense to have a leader go through a leadership development program when he or she is in the midst of some major change effort, our response is: That may well be the *best* time!

Timing

Each of the three factors just discussed (potential for advancement, transition, and organizational change/support) has something to do with timing. Either the leader going through the development experience saw an opportunity to advance in the foreseeable future, the leader was in the midst of some sort of professional transition, or the leader's organization was going through some sort of significant change.

Beyond those three factors, a number of our most improved leaders cited other timing-related factors that created a degree of ripeness. The most common example was when a leader had been in his or her role for one to three years. This, evidently, was long enough to have successfully gotten through a transition into the role, and also for their coworkers to have had ample opportunity to form valid impressions of the leader's style, strengths, and areas for improvement—and therefore to provide helpful feedback. And, at the same time, having been in the role no more than around three years created a context in which coworkers' perceptions of the leader had not yet hardened, such that good-faith efforts on the part of the leader to improve were especially likely to be well received.

Additionally, this amount of time seemed to be long enough to enable our leaders to form an accurate understanding of what they needed to do to lead more effectively, but not so long as to feel overly entrenched in their old ways of operating. In other words, the timing increased their ripeness by providing them with clarity or perspective about their potential evolution as a leader. Sufficient time in one's role serves to both enhance confidence and improve familiarity with the role, which likely drives the internal

RIPEN factor of Expectation. It also strikes us as very likely that sufficient time in role also promotes soul-searching and reflection, which relates to the internal RIPEN factor of Realization.

One of our most improved leaders, for example, had been in a Director-level position for about a year, noting that "you don't get trained for that—you just get put there." This leader said that during that year he had "played around" with some approaches to leading his team and that he knew he "needed to do some polishing." So, for him, the leadership development opportunity came at just the right time.

Other factors related to timing include key milestones (for example, a leader recently having turned a certain age), a change in the makeup of one's team (for example, the loss or acquisition of a key team member), and many other examples. In fact, we think that the importance of timing gets at the very essence of the "ripeness" analogy. If you eat a piece of fruit before it is ripe it will be hard and bitter; if you eat it when it is overly ripe it will be soft and mushy. Timing is, in short, extremely important, both when it comes to what we eat and also when it comes to how (and when) we develop our leaders.

The relationship between a leader's ripeness and timing is not limited only to leaders being riper at certain points in their career than at others. Our most improved leaders also suggested that they needed enough time or bandwidth to focus sufficiently on their development. In other words, some of our most improved leaders believed that not being overly inundated with day-to-day work responsibilities allowed them to get the most from the leadership development experience.

We believe that organizations implementing leadership development initiatives should keep this sort of thing in mind, and should think systematically about the importance of timing to facilitate a higher likelihood of improvement overall. Just as one of the leaders from our sample stated, "Maybe something to think about—it would be extremely difficult if you have your full-blown job commitment. If there is any way to lighten one's commitment a bit so that one can be really committed to this, that would be good."

Time and time again, we have seen that leaders feel they need to be wholeheartedly committed to actually changing their behavior while also ensuring that any changes are actually noticed by others. The two go hand in hand, and they often require a substantive amount of effort, time, and resources. This means that difficult decisions will have to be made about the allocation of limited time and resources. The implication is that organizations are well served to ensure that leaders participating in leadership development programs have sufficient bandwidth or capacity to reap the benefits of their involvement.

In summary, a variety of extrinsic (or "Outside In") factors, ranging from potential for advancement to organizational change to support from others, seem to have influenced our most improved leaders to be ripe for development. We have come to believe that such extrinsic ripeness factors are particularly important because of the impact that they have on an individual's intrinsic ripeness, as captured by the factors in the RIPEN model. Examples of this relationship between extrinsic and intrinsic ripeness factors have been provided throughout this chapter, but the basic logic is: An extrinsic ripeness factor (such as a specific promotion opportunity) must somehow appeal to a given leader's intrinsic motivators (such as the intrinsic ripeness factor of "ambition"), which in turn results in a level of ripeness that is predictive of actual improvement on the part of that leader.

For organizations that want to improve at assessing the ripeness of one or more leaders before investing in their development, Avion's RIPEN assessment provides insight both into the degree to which a given leader is ripe for development and also into specific RIPEN factors that may need to be addressed in order to create a high likelihood of improvement. Then coaches, managers, and entire organizations can tailor external ripeness factors to enhance the return on investment (ROI) of their development efforts. Of course, all of this simply means that a given leader is now ripe for improvement—which means it's time for the actual development to begin! And that is where we pick up in our next chapter.

Recommendations

For the Leader

- Seek out mentors who model the leadership behaviors you aspire to, or to whom you are comfortable opening up regarding your development challenges. Ask them if they will be a sounding board for you as you work on your action plan.

- Discuss your development needs, as identified through a 360-degree feedback process, with individuals in your personal life in order to better understand how these development needs show up in your personal life.

- During transitions, reflect upon what skills a transition into a new role will demand that you develop. Explore what strengths got you to where you are now and what skills you will need to develop in order to be successful in this specific role. Visualize or describe to a trusted confidant your desired evolution or development and what behaviors you will need to display in order to realize this growth.

- If your organization has a formal mentor program, use this as a way to get connected with someone to help you address your action plan.

For the Organization

- Ensure that the participant has the sufficient bandwidth or capacity to fully take advantage of the development experience.

- When appropriate or accurate, highlight that a specific leader is being considered for promotion into a specific role, depending on his or her ability to make specific changes in leadership style, and articulate to the leader the specific changes desired.

- Ensure that program content provides practical, on-the-job skills (e.g., if the organization is experiencing widespread change, ensure that the program incorporates change leadership content).

- Highlight the specific skills a leader will need to demonstrate in order to successfully transition into a new role.

- Build in periodic touch points with one's manager as a part of ongoing development initiatives in order to align learning experiences and motivational currency with the manager's expectations.

- Link participation in development initiatives with transitions and organizational changes.

- Link executive coaching with participation in classroom-based leadership development experiences.

- Embed, and publicize, the involvement of senior leaders in your development experiences to provide attendees with exposure to senior leaders.

- Get HR involved in the coaching process as internal advisors.

For the Coach

- Ask leaders you are working with questions that help them think about who else they should rely on to execute their leadership development plans.

- Explore the concerns of leaders you are working with regarding any transition into a new role (i.e., do they feel comfortable taking risks in modifying their behavior while transitioning into a new role, etc.).

- Establish clear expectations, with both the participant and his or her manager, regarding the time commitments associated with participation in an ongoing development program and ensure that the leader has sufficient time to fully capitalize on the benefit of the program.

- Provide objective and unbiased feedback regarding how the leader you are working with is performing in coaching sessions. Your objectivity is valued!

- Help the leader you are working with to craft personally relevant forms of leadership that address their feedback and the meet the organization's cultural needs. In other words, ensure that leaders are both making change on their own and evolving their own brand of leadership based on feedback from others.

CHAPTER FOUR

Central Issue

Over time, we started to notice something about the leaders we work with. Here's a typical scenario: We are working with a group of high-potential, high-performing leaders, and the work includes some leadership training, some 360-degree feedback, and some one-on-one leadership coaching. During the initial coaching meeting with a given leader, we work together on an action plan, which includes two to three strengths, two to three areas for development (more on how these are identified in Chapter 11), and action steps related to the areas for development.

Then, in the second coaching meeting a few weeks later, the coach asks the leader something like, "So, what are you working on?" And the answer is something like, "Uh, it's, uh . . . wait a minute . . . it's, uh—oh, it's in my action plan—where did I put that. . . ."

Our conclusion: If the leader can't even *recall* what he or she is working on, there's a pretty good chance he or she isn't really working on it.

Conversely, the most improved leaders in our study, when asked what they could recall about their action plans many months after developing them, almost invariably remembered *exactly* what they were working on. In addition, we noticed that they tended not to give us a list of areas for improvement; rather, they generally cited one or two key areas of focus—and, when there was more than one area of focus, the multiple areas generally were interrelated.

This finding led to our third key insight: The idea that leaders who improve significantly over time tend to focus on one key area for improvement—what we have started referring to as the central issue. Our conversations on this topic then led us to the question: How exactly would we define the term, *central issue*?

Merriam-Webster defines the word *central* as follows: "In the middle of something; located in the center of a thing or place; main or most important; controlling all other parts; having power over the other parts." Further, the first definition Merriam-Webster offers of the word *issue* is, in part, "an important subject or topic." So let's see how these dictionary definitions line up with what we found in our research.

Questions Related to the Central Issue

We found evidence of literally each aspect of the above definitions of the terms *central* and *issue* as we explored the nature and importance of the central issue as a factor that explained why our most improved leaders got better. More specifically, here are the factors that, based on our interviews, seem to characterize a central issue among our most improved leaders. We have framed the insights in this chapter as *five key questions* that leaders, or the coaches they work with, can ask to help identify one's central issue.

Does Feedback All Point in One Direction?

The first part of the definition of *central* indicates that it involves something being in the *middle* of something else. There is a particular way of referring to one's central issue that we heard in multiple interviews: the idea that "everything pointed to" that issue. In other words, when our most improved leaders read through all of their feedback, it seems that some of them—consciously or not—focused their improvement efforts on one issue that was "in the center" of all of the other feedback, and that all other feedback "pointed to," as illustrated in Figure 4.1.

Here is how one of our most improved leaders put it: "My key issue was taking actions to empower people on my team to own their areas of the business, to drive our respective business. *Everything pointed to that.*" This leader received a feedback report that was dozens of pages long, just like every other leader in our study. The feedback included average ratings on different leadership competencies and specific survey items, benchmark ratings to show how the leader compared with other leaders, written comments (both positive and developmental) from coworkers, and so on. But what this leader did—that not all leaders do—is figure out: What is all of this feedback *pointing* to?

In the case of this particular leader, there were several seemingly distinct themes in his feedback. There was a perception that he was not being sufficiently strategic for a leader at his level; there was a perception that he needed to invest more time in networking and relationship-building; there was a perception that he wasn't managing his time especially well; and there was a perception that his direct reports felt micro-managed at times.

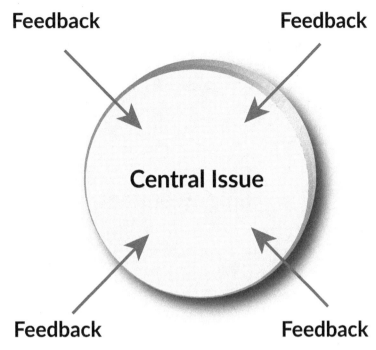

Figure 4.1

After reflecting on all of this feedback, he concluded that it was all pointing to the same basic issue: The need for him to empower his people more. Doing so would free up time to be more strategic and build stronger relationships, both within and outside of his organization. All of this meant that he would be managing his time more effectively as a leader at his level. And, of course, if he were to become more effective at empowering his people, they would be less likely to see him as micro-managing. And this, of course, has a number of positive implications for employee engagement, people's growth and development, and ultimately the productivity of that leader's department. (See Figure 4.2.)

In the same vein, one of our most improved leaders said that he saw several areas in his feedback in which he was above average, and several in which he was below average. So his approach was to focus on "one big area—public speaking." His thinking was that focusing on that area would help him improve in other areas, as well. As he put it, "public speaking is vital, even when building your network, for example, because if you are nervous to talk, you don't meet a lot of people."

This leader developed an action plan that included concrete steps that were intended to help him become more effective in situations in which he was expected to be the "lead communicator." For example, as a leader

Figure 4.2

who was responsible for a large geographic region of his company's operations within the United States, he held periodic conference calls with direct reports who were in different locations. He began preparing differently for those meetings, and he noticed that he was becoming more effective, which increased his confidence. Further, this led to increased comfort with having informal meetings with colleagues when he traveled to corporate headquarters, which resulted in improved networking.

In yet another example, a leader we were working with had received extensive 360-degree feedback, both qualitative and quantitative, in which there were literally hundreds of data points and dozens of comments. But during a discussion of the feedback with a coach, the leader immediately came to the conclusion that most of the specific developmental feedback was related. Specifically, this leader noticed that; "this all points to me needing to take my leadership to the next level. Almost all of this feedback tells me I am operating one level below where I should be—I am too involved in the day to day operations—so I need to elevate my approach in order to really be a better leader to my team."

In each of these examples, by focusing on the one thing that most everything else seemed to point toward, the leader directly addressed one key issue in his or her feedback (empowerment, public speaking, and operating at the right level) and also indirectly addressed several other issues. In this sense, there is actually a two-way relationship between feedback and one's central issue. In other words, many seemingly distinct bits of feedback may all point to the same central issue, and correspondingly, effectively addressing one's central issue should have a positive impact on those same, seemingly disparate themes within one's feedback.

To relate this back to the example cited above, we strongly suspect that if the leader's coworkers were to start associating the word *empowering* with that leader, then he would not only have addressed a specific theme in his feedback, he also would have affected a change in his approach to leadership that would have positive consequences for a range of other issues (strategic leadership, relationship-building, etc.). This is the power of the central issue.

Coincidentally, something directly related to the concept of the central issue happened while one of the authors was working on this chapter. The author was listening to a music-streaming service while writing, and a commercial came on with a male voice asking, "What one word would I want people to associate with me?" This caught the author's attention, because it is consistent with the idea of a leader's central issue (although the commercial was advertising something totally unrelated to leadership). The bottom line is that improvement requires focus.

What Is the Common Thread?

There is a different analogy that we heard about in our interviews: The analogy of the "common thread." Interestingly, if one does a search on the Internet using the phrase "common thread," one finds that few people bother to write about what a common thread actually is. It apparently has become so widely accepted as an analogy that there is now very little interest in where the analogy came from.

However, undaunted, one of the authors decided to personally get in touch with someone who would undoubtedly be an expert in the actual meaning of the term, *common thread*. The same Internet search that failed to produce a clear statement of the actual meaning of the term did turn up several establishments offering products and services related to fabrics and sewing, and a call was placed to one such establishment: A shop in Portland, Oregon, called "The Common Thread."

The owner of the shop, Laura, very kindly took a few minutes to indulge a stranger calling with an unusual question: "I am writing a book with some colleagues, we want to include a section on the notion of the 'common thread,' and we are wondering—what does the term actually mean?"

After reflecting on the question, Laura replied that, "in sewing, we use a common thread to gather fabric," and she noted that it's a "very important part of the construction of almost any garment." We think this actual meaning of the term *common thread* nicely captures the essence of what we heard from some of our most improved leaders: Their central issue was represented by some theme in their feedback that helped them to *gather together* all the other feedback into a single, concise issue they can work on.

An example from our interviews will further illustrate the idea of the common thread. One of our most improved leaders said, "What really came out as a common thread was that I needed to maintain my composure." And, indeed, one of the lowest-rated survey items in this leader's 360-degree feedback report was the survey item, "Maintains composure in stressful situations."

However, a review of the written comments portion of this leader's feedback report reveals that very few of his coworkers actually used the word "composure." Rather, they used words like "passion," "demeanor," "frustration," and "emotions" (as in, "he wears his emotions on his sleeve"). On reflection, though, these were really just different ways of getting at the same idea: This leader needed to improve in the area of composure. That was the word that seemed to best "gather together" most of the other developmental feedback this leader received. It was, for this leader, the common thread in his feedback.

This example illustrates three key points about the nature of the common thread. First, it underscores a truth that has become increasingly clear to us over time—the idea that true common threads often explain both strengths and weaknesses. In other words, sometimes the same behavior has different types of impact on different people. In fact, the leader who got feedback that he was too "emotional" also got feedback that he demonstrated great "passion." This can be both one's strength and one's weakness—sometimes all at once. The common thread in this case might be composure, defined as "*appropriate* displays of emotion."

The second key point that the composure example gets at is that it helps make the distinction between the common thread and the first factor that was cited above related to the central issue: Everything pointing to a single issue. Here's the difference. When a number of issues point to a single issue, they are fundamentally different issues, but by focusing on the central issue, the leader will also be positively impacting the other issues. In the example cited earlier, focusing on empowerment will help the leader simultaneously address several other issues (strategic thinking, relationship-building, and so on).

With the common thread, on the other hand, the feedback is not really suggesting that an issue is one's central issue because focusing on it will drive improvement in other, related areas. Rather, the common thread refers to a single issue that is described in a number of different ways—but it's all basically the same issue. Said differently, one behavior can have a number of impacts or manifestations or can impact different people differently. Think of taking the most important areas of feedback and distilling them into one focus area—this is idea behind the common thread. In the composure example described above, that was the key issue for the leader; people just used different ways of describing it.

Which leads to the third key point that the composure example gets at. As we will see in later chapters, one of the keys to improvement is the way in which a leader goes back and discusses his or her feedback with people who provided the feedback. And we believe that one important consideration is the wording that one chooses to capture an area for development (whether a strength to build on or a relative weakness to address).

To stick with the composure example, this leader could have gone back and told people, "Well, based on my feedback, I clearly need to stop yelling at people when I get stressed out." Here's why we think "composure" is a better way of framing this issue. For starters, we think it's just more descriptive, professional language, which we believe is a plus when describing behavior in the workplace—whether others' or one's own. In addition, it's more succinct; it takes a whole sentence and boils it down to one word, which likely makes it easier for the leader to keep in the front of his or her mind. Which, incidentally, leads us to the next factor related to the central issue.

What Message Becomes Front of Mind?

The thing that initially caused us to identify the question of what becomes "front of mind" as another factor related to the idea of the central issue is that a number of our most improved leaders used that very phrase. For example, the leader cited above who was primarily working on empowerment said, "My key issue was taking actions to empower people on my team to own their areas of the business, to drive our respective business. This was front of mind."

Similarly, another leader cited several interrelated areas for development, and then said, "Presentation skills, leadership presence, showcasing the team in (my manager's) meetings—these were all front of mind." This quote gets at both the idea that there may be a *common thread* that gathers together several related issues and also that it's important for the leader to have a way of keeping his or her central issue in the front of his or her mind.

Any leadership development professional who has worked in the area of emotional intelligence is probably aware that we all have *frontal lobes,* in the frontal and upper area of one's cortex, which is a part of our brain that carries out higher-level mental processes such as thinking, decision-making, and planning. So, in a sense, keeping something front of mind is literally accurate: Hopefully, one's central issue does help drive our thoughts, decisions, and plans.

However, perhaps a better way to get our minds around the importance of identifying a central issue that one can keep front of mind comes from the world of marketing. In that field, the phrase "front-of-mind awareness" (also referred to as "top-of-mind awareness") refers to a measure of how readily a brand name or concept comes to people's minds. In other words, front-of-mind awareness has been achieved when a specific brand or product comes to mind first when consumers think about a specific industry.

To illustrate, when one thinks about the word *tissue,* what specific brand comes to mind first for most of us? The word that probably came immediately to mind is *Kleenex,* which is actually a brand, not a type of product. But that particular brand has achieved such "front-of-mind awareness" that it is almost universally associated with tissue.

We believe that when a leader frames something as a central issue, it has a similar effect. A typical leader receiving 360-degree feedback will be taking in all sorts of messages, much as the typical consumer watching TV or surfing the Internet will be taking in all sorts of messages, and much as the typical voter will be vaguely aware that there are a whole bunch of candidates trying to get people to vote for him or her. A good marketer knows that one key to selling his or her product is cutting through all the clutter and getting that product to come to mind first for consumers, much as a good political consultant knows that one key to getting votes is cutting through all the clutter and getting one's candidate to come to mind first for voters.

All of this has at least a couple of implications for leaders who improve. First, it is important to note that one of the things that characterized the central issue for some of our most improved leaders was that the issue was something that was front of mind for these leaders, even months after they had gotten their feedback and developed their action plans. Second, we believe it's possible for leaders to proactively and deliberately do some things in order to make it more likely that one's central issue will remain front of mind. More will be said about this later; suffice it to say for now that another factor that makes an issue a *central* issue is that it becomes and remains front of mind for the leader.

What Blind Spots Get Exposed?

Intuitively, one might think that a leader's central issue would be in an area that especially resonates with the leader—perhaps because it is in an area in which the leader has previously received feedback that he or she needs to improve. However, this is generally not what we found to be the case.

To the contrary, one of the factors that characterizes the central issues that our most improved leaders identified is that they were in areas in which the leaders were *surprised* that they were getting feedback that they needed to become more effective. Here are a couple of examples.

One of our most improved leaders said, "My central issue was collaboration," and she went on to explain that, "this was my central issue because I was surprised by it." The reason she was surprised by her feedback in that area was that she had gotten positive feedback in that very area and actually thought of "collaboration" as one of her key strengths, rather than as an area for improvement. To see lower-rated survey items and somewhat critical written comments in that area was startling to her. This leader went on to explain that, "Because I would have thought it was a strength of mine, I was especially motivated to want to improve."

Another of our most improved leaders, who had a completely different central issue, nonetheless expressed a similar sentiment. As this leader put it, "It's pretty powerful when people you work with daily clearly think you need to work on something but they never say it, and the 360 was a way of finding this out."

Yet another example involved one of our most improved leaders getting feedback from his manager indicating that he needed to improve in the area of problem-solving. At first this was surprising to the leader, as he had always viewed problem-solving as one of his key strengths. However, as he thought more deeply about the feedback, he decided that the issue was that, in his words, "I kept these skills to myself, meaning that I would solve a problem but not share that with anybody." So his central issue became communication—appropriately and effectively letting people know about solutions he had come up with.

We think these last few examples illustrate a couple of key ideas when it comes to the nature and importance of the central issue. First, we think they illustrate the way in which all of these insights into how leaders improve are interrelated. For example, in Chapters 2 and 3 we talked about "ripeness" as being critical to improvement. As all three of the examples just cited illustrate, surprising feedback can make a leader "ripe" for improvement (or "motivated," as the leader in one of the above examples put it).

Put differently, all of the insights we are sharing throughout this book form a mosaic, in which the specific pieces work together to create a picture of the leader who is highly likely to actually get better. For the leader reading this book who desires to improve, we encourage you to take a step back and ask questions like: Does this mosaic look like me? In general, am I the kind of leader that has just been described? Are these the kinds of reactions I tend to have to feedback? Are these the sorts of actions I tend to take in response to feedback? In short, the whole is greater than the sum of the parts; while the individual insights are important, the key is to approach personal improvement with the essence of what is described throughout. As one of the authors emphasizes to the people he coaches, the goal in interpreting feedback is to listen to the music, not just the individual notes.

A popular model called the Johari Window effectively captures the other key idea that last few examples illustrate. The model, created by two American psychologists, Joseph Luft and Harrington Ingham, is intended to help people, including leaders, to better understand both themselves and others. The model consists of four quadrants: Things that are known to self, things that are unknown to self, things that are known to others, and things that are unknown to others,[1] as shown in Figure 4.3.

Each of the four quadrants in this model can serve as a very useful way of talking about a leader's feedback; however, the quadrant that relates to

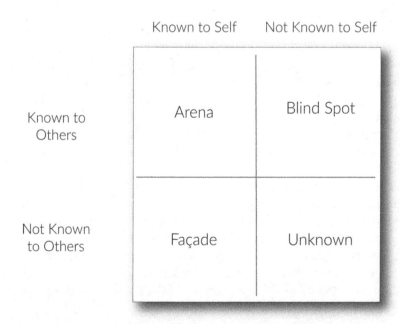

Figure 4.3

the current discussion is the "known to others but unknown to self" quadrant—otherwise known as the "Blind Spot." The leader cited above who thought she was particularly strong in the area of collaboration and then saw that some of her lowest-rated 360-degree feedback items were in that area had a Blind Spot exposed. That which was previously known to others and unknown to self had now moved into the quadrant of the Johari Window known as the "Arena," where something is known both to others and to self.

As we sometimes say to leaders we work with, "The feedback doesn't create the perception." The perception was already there; the feedback just brings it out into the open. It's a gift, and the leader receiving the feedback can choose what he or she wants to do with that gift—including choosing to do nothing at all.

However, the option of doing nothing at all brings us to another concept from the field of psychology: The concept of "cognitive dissonance"— the discomfort someone may feel when he or she holds two or more contradictory beliefs, ideas, or values at the same time.[2]

To go back to the example of the leader who identified collaboration as her central issue, the concept of cognitive dissonance would work as follows. On one hand, the leader clearly seemed to value being seen as someone who was collaborative, stating that she had always seen that as one of her strengths. Yet here was feedback (from people she respected, it should be stressed) indicating that she actually was not seen as particularly strong in that area.

This created cognitive dissonance, and upon receiving that feedback, the leader in this example essentially had two options: (a) start thinking differently about collaboration (for example, "it's actually not that important in this job"); or (b) change people's perceptions of her ability to collaborate so that it was once again in alignment with her belief that collaboration is indeed important. This leader chose option B, and indeed, she made it her central issue. And, of course, she ended up being one of our most improved leaders.

Can I Really Control This?

Here's a scenario. Suppose that you are the new Chief Human Resources Officer for a large pharmaceutical company and upon getting your first 360-degree feedback report, you read feedback saying that you are not seen as really understanding the science behind the drugs in your company's pipeline. Further, suppose that you have spent your entire career up to that point in the financial services industry (not the pharmaceutical industry).

While you may acknowledge that you need to do some things to get up the learning curve more quickly in terms of your company's core mission and products, it probably would not make sense for you to come up with an action plan that is specifically geared toward being in the top 10% within the company on the survey item, "Understands the science behind the drugs in (company's) pipeline." First, it's probably not realistic. And second, even if it were possible, it would probably be a terrible use of your time and energy.

This is perhaps an extreme example (although not that big a departure from some of our actual experiences for clients we have served). However, it illustrates another factor that tended to characterize our most improved leaders' central issues. To go back to the leader who identified collaboration as her central issue, part of the rationale, as she expressed it to us, was that "I had control over it; it was based on what I did; I owned all of that myself."

Once again, there is a term from the field of psychology (also cited earlier in the chapter on intrinsic ripeness) that explains why this factor is important: Self-efficacy. This simply refers to the extent of one's belief in his or her ability to complete tasks and reach goals.[3]

For example, I may have very little self-efficacy when it comes to really learning the science behind drugs in my company's pipeline if I am an HR professional in my mid-50s who has spent my entire career in a completely different industry. So, even if the feedback stings, I am not very inclined to make it my central issue because it doesn't resonate with me as something I can actually change.

On the other hand, I may have a great deal of self-efficacy when it comes to being more collaborative—regardless of my function or background. So, if my feedback exposes a blind spot and my reaction is to say, "Yeah—I can fix that," then I have latched onto an issue that may well be a great candidate to serve as my *central issue*. At least, it appears that this is how our most improved leaders approached it.

What Is My Development Focus?

Given that leaders are often preoccupied with other responsibilities, they have to find time to integrate their development goals and actions to maximize their efficiency. One of the likely reasons that central issues were so common among our most improved leaders is that they created focus for one's development efforts.

More specifically, having a central issue enables a leader to, in essence, use a relatively broad lens through which to view a number of disparate bits of feedback in order to focus on a consistent theme. For example, one

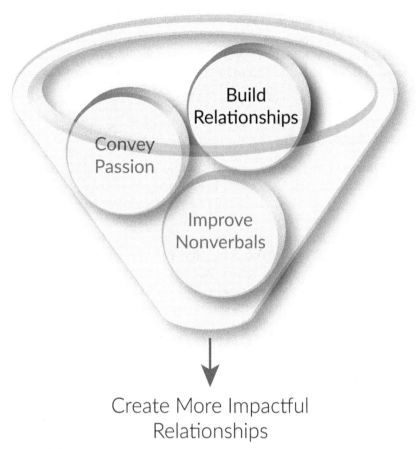

Figure 4.4

of our most improved leaders wanted to work on both building relationships and conveying passion. This leader integrated these two specific development goals under the central issue of "Creating More Impactful Relationships," illustrated in Figure 4.4. The leader's action steps included networking, meeting one on one with others in the organization, and seeking to use effective nonverbal and verbal forms of communication.

Another leader we worked with, who had recently been promoted to an expanded role, was encouraged through the feedback process to develop a more strategic view of the business (because the leader had previously been so focused on deep expertise within a particular product line) *and* to improve in the area of "leading leaders" (as opposed to just leading technical experts, which had been the leader's previous focus). In this case, the leader focused on the central issue of "Growing from Technical Leader to Functional Leader," which drove key behavior changes required in the leader's new, elevated role.

In each of the examples cited in the last few paragraphs, the leader identified a central issue from different pieces of feedback that originally addressed different topic areas—but which, when combined, actually gave unified and focused attention to an area of development that helped the leader to improve significantly.

Common Central Issues

One question we have sought to answer thus far in this chapter is: What are the *factors* that characterize a central issue? We have framed these factors as five key questions to ask in order to determine what a given leader's central issue might be.

Another question that intrigued us, once we had gathered all of our data, was: What are some *common* central issues? This was actually a fairly simple question to answer, as the leaders we interviewed generally indicated exactly what their central issues were. Indeed, as mentioned at the outset of this chapter, the fact that one's central issue came immediately to mind is one of the things that we believe resulted in these leaders being in the "most improved leader" group, and we believe that having a clear central issue is something that should be taught as a best practice of leaders who actually improve.

When we went through our data to determine what the most common central issues were, we found two extremely interesting things. First, by far the most common central issue was some variation of communication. Now this took many forms, including giving feedback, receiving feedback, presentation skills, one-on-one conversations, listening, expressiveness, and others. But the common thread, so to speak, running through all of these central issues is that they all have something to do with communication. In fact, roughly one-third of all of the central issues identified by our most improved leaders seemed to fall into the category of communication effectiveness.

The second very interesting thing we found can be illustrated by this list of actual central issues from our most improved leaders (categorized in a way that we think makes sense and listed in alphabetical order):

- Adapting Leadership Style
- Business Acumen
- Collaboration
- Communication
- Composure

- Developing Talent
- Driving Execution
- Empathy
- Empowerment
- Leadership Presence
- Networking
- Relationship-building
- Strategic Leadership

One thing about this list probably becomes immediately apparent to the reader: Virtually all of these central issues have something to do with what are often referred to as "soft skills." True, there arguably are a few exceptions (business acumen, driving execution, strategic leadership). However, it seems clear that nontechnical competencies dwarf more technical competencies when it comes to our most improved leaders' central issues.

While we think this is an important finding with significant implications for leadership development, it is probably not very surprising to anyone who is familiar with the research in the area of Emotional Intelligence. Daniel Goleman and other thought leaders in that field have for years been citing research that clearly indicates that nontechnical competencies (the proverbial "soft skills") are much better predictors of leadership effectiveness than technical competencies (the proverbial "hard skills").[4] In other words, our study represents one more bit of data to suggest that focusing on soft skills is critical when it comes to leadership development.

Recommendations

For the Leader

- Assume that some of your feedback that seems unrelated may actually be sending you the same message, or at least related messages. Even if it's not obvious at first, applying this method may illuminate a central issue you had not noticed at first.
- Analyze your most consistent strength and development areas, and ask yourself what the common denominator is between these two areas.
- Try to narrow your primary area for development down to a single word, phrase, or short sentence that you can easily remember and repeat.
- Think about how previous feedback you have received relates to your current feedback, and ask, "Are there similarities or themes across time?" Often

there are. If so, use that broader set of "data" to draw from as you try to synthesize those inputs into a single central issue.

- Do root-cause analysis to see if feedback is all related to some sort of common cause.
- Determine if one action, or similar types of actions, can address multiple developmental messages.

For the Organization

- Identify high-frequency central issues within your organization and offer targeted skill-building sessions in these areas.
- Recognize and address the possibility that if there are thematic central issues across leaders within the organization, senior leaders' modeling of behaviors and the company's culture may be largely responsible for these common central issues.
- Pair up individuals with strengths in areas that correspond to others' central issues, thereby creating mentoring opportunities.
- Offer group reflection sessions comprised of participants with similar central issues who can learn from each other and share wisdom with the broader organization.
- If similar central issues continue to surface over time, consider factors such as selection criteria, training and development approaches, and other human-resources–related variables as a possible explanation.

For the Coach

- If a leader does not self-identify a central issue, look to help the leader to do so by examining data to identify either a common thread (where various data support the same conclusion) or different themes that may all be addressed by focusing on some other central issue.
- Unless absolutely critical to address, shift the leader's attention away from feedback that is not related to the central issue, since leaders often get distracted by one-off comments or low scores on survey items that have a low correlation to their overall success (in other words, if it's not a critical issue and it's not connected to the central issue, then encourage the leader to deprioritize that feedback, or even ignore it).
- When working with a leader to create a written action plan, build in an area to capture the leader's central issue (in fact, encourage each leader to focus on action planning relative to one's central issue, and not on the broader panoply of feedback received).
- Reframe messages in a way that forces the leader to look at issues from a different perspective.

CHAPTER FIVE

Penetrating Message

The impetus for considering whether a "penetrating message" in one's 360-degree feedback might be a critical factor in how leaders improve came not from a leadership development program, but rather from personal experience, once again from one of the authors. Here is the story, in the author's own words.

> As a father of three children, all of whom were heavily involved in sports, I spent many seasons coaching my kids' baseball and soccer teams. In all, I spent 13 consecutive years coaching my kids' teams. And, combined with my professional duties, responsibilities as a husband, and various other commitments (to my church, etc.), I simply did not make time to work out. And I rationalized this by telling myself that I was keeping active and reasonably fit through all the time I was spending on my kids' baseball and soccer fields. And there actually was at least some truth to this.
>
> But then, several years ago, I coached my last season—my second son's ninth year of Little League baseball. And then soon after that, I got some feedback—in the form of what I now refer to as a "penetrating message."
>
> Around the time of my last season coaching, I was in my mid-40s and my wife had convinced me that I needed to start going to the doctor for annual check-ups. So, I did. And my physician asked me some questions about my lifestyle. Was I a smoker? No. Do I drink alcohol? Yes—in moderation. How much do I exercise? I answered honestly. And then he recorded a word in my medical records. I honestly don't remember whether he told me what the word was, or whether I saw him writing it. But I remember very clearly exactly what the word was: "Sedentary."
>
> This was several years ago, and I still vividly remember the impact that word had on me. While I had not belonged to a gym for roughly two decades, and while I had not been an active runner or anything like that

since probably my first couple years in college, I certainly did not consider myself sedentary. But my physician is an expert in translating behavior into impact, and his label for my behavior was "sedentary."

And that was not OK with me. It was not a word I ever wanted anyone to use when describing me. So, with some encouragement from my wife, our whole family joined a gym. And, with some encouragement from a close friend, I took up mountain biking. And I started regularly hiking Cowles Mountain in San Diego—the highest point in the city of San Diego at 1,594 feet.

Today, at age 53, nobody would confuse me with an Olympic athlete. I could still afford to lose a good 20 pounds and a couple inches off my waist size. However, when I was at the doctor about a week before the writing of this chapter, a Physician's Assistant took my pulse and blood pressure and asked me the sweetest of questions: "Are you an avid runner?"

This was another penetrating message, this time in the form of a question. And strong encouragement to continue getting into the gym on regular basis!

This personal experience prompted us to wonder: When leaders get 360-degree feedback, and when they then improve dramatically, is it at least sometimes the case that there was a single, penetrating message in their feedback that caused them to really stand up and take notice? To really grasp, perhaps for the first time, that a significant change in behavior was critical?

Allow us to cite one more personal example. In the spirit of practicing what one preaches, most of this book's authors have gone through 360-degree feedback multiple times. One of us still vividly recalls, verbatim, a specific written comment from a 360-degree feedback report—one that was received roughly 20 years ago: "Not a team player."

Ouch. For someone who very much values being a team player and wants to be seen that way, this particular bit of feedback really stung. This author made it a goal from that point on not just to be as much of a team player as possible, but also to hopefully not do anything that would create any sort of a perception to the contrary. And while this author has received his fair share of development feedback since then (both in person and in the eight 360-degree surveys he participated in subsequent to that initial survey), he never again saw that particular phrase, or any close variation of it, in one of his own 360 reports.

A typical 360 report consists of both a quantitative section (numeric ratings on dozens of specific survey items, as well as on the broader categories into which they fall) and a qualitative section (verbatim written comments in response to two or more open-ended questions). And, depending on the number of people who complete the survey, the comments alone may be several pages long.

In other words, there are lots of data in a typical 360-degree feedback report. And it can be a challenge for a leader reading through such a report to know what to attend to. This, of course, is part of the value of having a leader work with a skilled leadership coach as a part of the leadership development process.

Sometimes, though, a leader keys in on a particular comment—a word or a phrase—and it's clear that that particular bit of feedback is going to be the catalyst for change. Our question was: Is this tendency to key in on a memorable comment or phrase common among the leaders who improve the most? As we analyzed our data and reflected on our own experiences, our answer was an unequivocal "yes." So we endeavored to figure out exactly what it is about a given bit of feedback that causes it to be a penetrating message.

The Nature of Penetrating Messages

Once it became clear to us that one predictor of whether a leader would improve significantly was some sort of penetrating message, we asked ourselves two questions: First, *Why* are penetrating messages so important? And second, What *type* of feedback tends to be construed as a penetrating message for a leader?

In exploring why penetrating messages were so pervasive among our most improved leaders, we reflected back on our experience as executive coaches. We believe that penetrating messages were associated with our most improved leaders for two important reasons. To begin with, in a typical 360-degree feedback experience, leaders tend to get a wide range of feedback, only a small portion of which may be truly memorable or penetrating for them. In some instances, a leader getting feedback receives one particularly salient or memorable piece of feedback that really grabs the leader's attention and serves to focus the leader's efforts over an extended period of time, as illustrated in Figure 5.1.

Second, we believe that penetrating messages were so prevalent among our most improved leaders because they jolted the individual to abandon their status quo and motivated them to embrace new ways of leading or behaving. Said differently, if you were to ask someone what his or her developmental goals are and he or she could not articulate them clearly and consistently, it is unlikely that this individual would be sufficiently motivated to sustain the focus and discipline necessary to make meaningful

Range of feedback received
by an individual

The single
penetrating
message

- ▲ "Should delegate more"
- ▲ "Could listen a bit better"
- ▲ "Not a team player"
- ▲ "Please set clearer expectations"
- ▲ "Work on public speaking"
- ▲ "Should continue to set a high bar for others"

"Not a team player"

Figure 5.1

behavior changes. This individual may intellectually know that change would be beneficial but would not keep this in mind on an ongoing basis during a typical workday. The message wouldn't have the salience necessary for this leader to catch him- or herself when he or she started to engage in the status quo behavior.

For example, one individual we coached received the tough feedback that "although not often observed, when others see the scintilla of humanity within you, they react favorably." A total of 26 feedback interviews were conducted on this leader's behalf and were synthesized into a 15-page summary document, and the one message the leader routinely came back to in our coaching was "scintilla of humanity." As you can imagine, this message was simultaneously shocking, troubling, and offensive to the individual who received it. However, upon deeper reflection, the recipient acknowledged that there was some truth to it (although he highlighted the very valid reasons why he felt he needed to be so tough and results-oriented). This penetrating message provided the leader with a memorable area to focus on ("show my softer side to others"), and it motivated consistent, long-term action ("I value both people *and* results, and I need to display my warmth and care for others more regularly").

Cognitive dissonance, a term introduced by the social psychologist Leon Festinger and mentioned in the previous chapter, refers to the mental stress or discomfort experienced by a person who simultaneously holds two or more contradictory beliefs, ideas, or values; who performs an action that contradicts those beliefs, ideas, or values; or who is confronted with new information that contradicts existing beliefs, ideas, and values.[1] In other words, as humans we strive to behave in cognitively consistent manners around our core beliefs and values, and when we don't it causes us angst. It seems likely that penetrating messages may motivate behavior change because of the cognitive dissonance they may trigger.

If we consider the "scintilla of humanity" example referenced above, this leader tended to be a tough, decisive, and results-oriented leader who valued a "zero defect work environment." He was proud to set high standards for himself and the large department that reported to him. In fact, multiple feedback providers noted that he was likely the best at his particular functional area in the entire industry. However, the perception that he was not regularly behaving in a warm or humane manner caused cognitive dissonance for him that resulted in both clarity about what he wanted to change, as well as sufficient internal motivation for him to take meaningful and ongoing action (Figure 5.2). In fact, six months after receiving his initial feedback, he received a follow-up feedback assessment, and he was very gratified to see that the perceptions that others held of him had changed significantly. In summary, penetrating messages are predictive of improvement among leaders because they create and reflect both the focus and motivation necessary to sustain meaningful behavior change over an extended period of time.

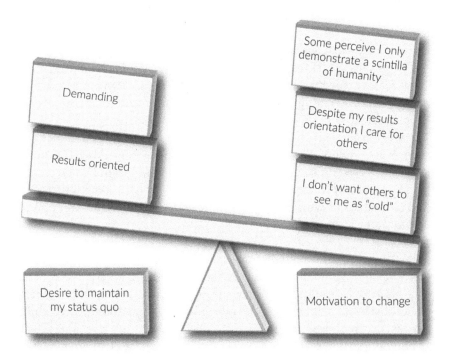

Figure 5.2

In terms of what *type* of feedback tends to be construed as a penetrating message, what struck us immediately was that there are several factors that did *not* seem to clearly delineate between a particularly penetrating message and all of the other messages that a leader normally receives during a typical leadership development process.

We found that sometimes a message is penetrating in part because it's a surprise. For example, one of our most improved leaders said she remembered getting feedback from her peers that she needed to keep a "tighter rein" on her direct reports, and she went on to say, "I had not gotten that feedback before, and the fact that I hadn't heard it before is one reason it stuck with me."

On the other hand, we found that sometimes a message is penetrating in part because it's *not* a surprise. One of our most improved leaders, for instance, said, "One of the key messages in my feedback was that I needed to be more strategic, and part of why I recall that is because I think I knew it; the feedback served as validation." This suggests that some penetrating messages may remind us of what we already believe to be true about ourselves.

Another example of a factor that did not clearly distinguish between a penetrating message and all the other feedback a leader may have gotten was the *source* of the feedback. For some leaders, the penetrating message came from a direct report, such as the leader who said that one comment that struck a nerve for her was a comment from a direct report, in which the feedback provider described the leader as "aloof" and said that leader "didn't always greet people" the way the leader should. This leader said, "That really made me think about how others perceive me in a group setting," and that seeming aloof "may not be what I mean to do, but it's how people perceived me."

For other leaders, the penetrating message came from one's manager, such as the leader who said that a key message he remembered from his feedback was a comment from his manager that he "needed to do a better job of prioritizing among the many good ideas" he had, something that he said he knew, but which served as both "a compliment and an opportunity for improvement."

For still other leaders, the penetrating message came from a peer, such as the leader mentioned earlier who said the feedback that most stuck out to her was the comment from a peer about needing to keep a "tighter rein" over her people. Another said that the key message he remembered from his feedback was a comment from one of his peers questioning his "ability to consistently communicate my ideas effectively at that level and above."

Finally, for some leaders, the penetrating message was not in one's feedback report at all. Rather, it came from the *coach* that the leader was working with. One of our most improved leaders illustrated this possibility with the following quote: "When my coach said, 'Sam (name changed), you carry yourself better than most executives,' that really stuck with me." And, as will be explored later in this chapter, as leadership coaches we have frequently gotten the sense that something we said in a coaching session really struck a chord with a leader and helped the leader make real progress in terms of his or her effectiveness—either by helping the leader build on a strength or by helping the leader address some relative weakness. In short, a penetrating message can come from almost any direction.

Another thing we wondered, as a result of examples like the ones just cited, was whether penetrating messages tended to pertain more to one's strengths or to one's relative weaknesses. Once again, we found no clear pattern, which was very surprising to us. Our experience is that most leaders we work with tend to hear the positive messages in their feedback reports as whispers and the negative messages as shouts.

As such, we fully expected that the vast majority of penetrating messages would be negative or developmental in nature. Perhaps because most of the leaders in our sample were participating in a high-potential leadership development program, this hypothesis was not borne out by the data. For instance, one leader noted that, "The key message for me was that I was good at relationship-building and communication, which resonated with me since I had heard this before from my leadership." On the other hand, one of our leaders said, "I got feedback that I don't communicate well, and my reaction was that I guess I thought I was better via e-mail and text than I apparently was."

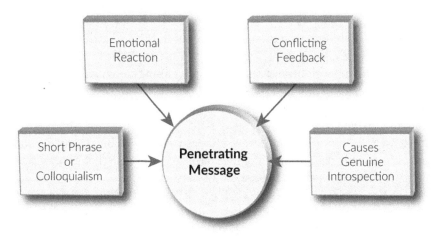

Figure 5.3

In short, we have thus far learned the following: Penetrating messages are sometimes surprising to the leader receiving them, and they are sometimes *not* so surprising; they may come from the leader's direct reports, peers, manager, or leadership coach; and they can pertain either to one's strengths or to one's relative weaknesses. So, if these are factors that do *not* really distinguish between penetrating messages and all the rest of the feedback that a leader may be getting, what *does* tend to characterize a penetrating message? Well, a few things—four, to be exact (Figure 5.3).

Short Phrase or Colloquialism

The first and perhaps most obvious thing we noticed about the messages that leaders found most penetrating is that often there was a short phrase—sometimes even a colloquialism—that was used by the feedback provider to convey a message. For example, one leader was told that she needed to keep a "tighter rein" on her people. We think this is an especially rich example for a few reasons, so we elaborate on it later in this chapter (and also in the next chapter on the idea of the "guiding metaphor"). Suffice it to say for now that this short phrase really caught the leader's attention. There were, however, other examples from our most improved leaders.

Another of our most improved leaders said that a penetrating message from his feedback was that he needed to better understand the "nuts and bolts" of what his people did. The message this leader took from this feedback was that he needed to have a better grasp of the implications of what he might ask a direct report to do in a given situation, and he said that feedback really "rang true." In response to this feedback, the leader said, "Now I stop and think: what are all steps this person is going to have to take to do this?"

Yet another leader said the message that really struck a chord with him involved use of the term *status quo*. As he put it, "I recall a comment about my department remaining status quo," and the insight this created for him was that, while he felt he and his team were making improvements in their area, these improvements were not shared more broadly outside the team. As a result, he said, "The phrase 'status quo' led to my action plan regarding showcasing the team and its successes." That message apparently really stuck with him and helped him to change his approach to ensuring that not only was his team improving the status quo, but also that he was making sure his team was getting the credit they deserved.

One final example of this idea came from a senior finance leader whose feedback said she needed to do a better job of "creating a team with bench strength." She noted that this feedback surfaced not only in her survey ratings, but in her written comments as well. Her reaction was, "That one kind of hit me hard, because I thought that was sort of a reflection on the leader." In other words, for her, it went to the heart of what a senior leader should be doing, and she determined that she was going to step up her efforts to ensure that her people were growing and developing and that she was also grooming a successor.

So, keeping a tighter rein on people, better understanding the nuts and bolts of what direct reports do, being stuck in the status quo, not developing bench strength—these are examples of specific penetrating messages that prompted actual change on the part of the leaders who received these messages. They are short and they are generally well-known phrases, likely thereby enabling them to be memorable and applicable to a broad range of behavior. But not every short, well-known phrase is necessarily a penetrating message. At a minimum, based on our research, the next condition is important, as well.

Emotional Reaction

A penetrating message, quite simply, creates some sort of emotional reaction. One of our most improved leaders offered a perfect example of this, saying, "Some comments about me not being attentive to people and not being in stores as much as I should be hurt my feelings; that message hit home." It should be noted that this comment came from a male leader in a company that has possibly the least warm and fuzzy culture any of us has ever worked in. So, our guess is that this leader is probably not especially prone to talking about having his feelings hurt. Further, the feedback was not framed in an unusually critical or disrespectful manner. But it seems like the core message—pay more attention to your people—resonated with this leader on an emotional, not just a rational, level and likely triggered some cognitive dissonance.

This tendency of penetrating messages to trigger emotional reactions was true for positive messages, as well as for more critical messages. One leader explained that the one thing that really surprised her was that, while she was expecting to get a positive report, she was surprised at *how* positive it was. She said that, "Even in areas where I expected the feedback to be worse, it was really good," and that, "the impact this had on me was that it made me feel better about myself."

This finding that penetrating messages tend to impact leaders emotionally, not just rationally, reminds us of two different forms of support for this phenomenon—one ancient and one contemporary. Anyone who has ever studied ancient Greek philosophy probably learned about Aristotle's three modes of influence: Ethos, Logos, and Pathos. Ethos essentially refers to the credibility of the source of an influence attempt. Logos refers to the rationality of an argument. And, of course, pathos refers to the emotional content of some appeal.[2]

We think all three of these modes of influence are important when it comes to feedback regarding one's effectiveness as a leader. The credibility of the source of some feedback is certainly important, as is the logical coherence of the message. But what our research suggests is that pathos, or feedback that prompts some sort of emotional response on the part of the leader, is especially likely to be a penetrating message and to motivate ongoing and consistent behavior change.

The second form of support comes the Center for Creative Leadership (CCL). David Baldwin and Curt Grayson identified three different types of influence tactics: logical, emotional, and cooperative.[3] These authors then noted that, based on research done at CCL, all three forms of influence are important in order to gain true commitment to any goal. So, even though we all tend to rely heavily on rational appeals in the organizational context, emotional appeals are also critically important. And, based on our research, it seems clear that the emotional aspect of a penetrating message helps explain why it creates a high level of commitment to improvement on the part of the leader receiving such a message.

In short, our study reinforces what ancient philosophers and contemporary organizational scholars have long known: Rational persuasion is merely one form of influence, and it may actually be far less effective than more emotional appeals. In our study, at least, one thing that characterized penetrating messages was that they struck an emotional chord.

Conflicting Feedback

We noted earlier that there was not a clear theme in terms of whether penetrating messages were surprising or whether they served to validate a self-perception that the leader already had. However, we did find that sometimes a message was particularly penetrating because the leader was getting two seemingly conflicting bits of feedback at the same time, each from a different type of coworker.

Sometimes, the two bits of seemingly contradictory feedback came from one's manager versus others. For example, one of our most improved leaders said, "Ronald (name changed) said I needed to be more strategic, which stuck out because others in my feedback said I WAS strategic." What this leader said next in the interview was enormously important. He declared, "That makes you want to go figure out—what is that person not seeing?" He then added that he and his manager then had a number of conversations about that over the course of the [leadership development] program."

As an important aside, this reaction to feedback beautifully illustrates one difference between the mindset of leaders who improve significantly and those who don't. We have been in many meetings over the years with leaders who get a feedback report, point to two different written comments in the report, and say, in a very defensive tone of voice, "Look, this feedback is contradictory" (or something to that effect).

For starters, this is very easily explained. We normally just say, very calmly, that the two comments came from two different people, and it's very common for two different people to have different perceptions of the same leader. We then explore possible explanations. For example, the leader may actually be behaving differently toward the two people who provided the feedback. Or perhaps the leader is behaving in a way that is quite consistent, but maybe the two people providing the feedback react differently to the behavior because they have different needs, personalities, and so on. Generally, the leader comes around and it turns into a productive conversation.

What is telling about the leader in this example, though, is that his initial feedback was *not* defensive. As he noted, this penetrating message from his manager caused the leader to wonder why his manager did not see him as strategic when others did. And it resulted in some great conversations with his manager and, ultimately, significant improvement on the part of the leader who was getting the feedback.

Another typical kind of conflicting feedback is between oneself and others. One of our leaders illustrated this with the following comment: "The first thing I remember thinking about my feedback was that I may have been a little over-confident." This leader elaborated, saying, "My self-scores were higher than others' scores in general," and he added that, "the impact that had on me was that it opened my eyes to the fact that I needed to do a better job of explaining the big picture." As with the first example, the key here is that the leader did not react defensively; rather, the response was to ask, "How do I need to think or act differently in order to close the gap here?" That focus and motivation was a theme across the leaders who got conflicting feedback and who improved.

Genuine Introspection

A fourth factor that we found to be characteristic of a penetrating message was that it created some sort of genuine introspection. In fact, we believe this factor, arguably, is the most important one in distinguishing between messages that are merely *noteworthy* and those that are truly *penetrating*. Two examples cited by our most improved leaders nicely illustrate this factor.

One example involves a human resources leader with a good sense of humor. We know he is funny, because one of us served as this leader's coach, and his intelligent and somewhat dry sense of humor often surfaced in our one-on-one conversations. When he got his feedback report, though, he found one message to be especially penetrating. In his words, that message was, "Not everything is a joke." That got his attention.

It caused him to become reflective, and he concluded that, "I tend to use humor when we are in stressful situations, which works for a lot of people, but not everyone." After some introspection, he made a decision that this was a part of his basic style in the workplace that needed at least an adjustment. And, nearly a year after receiving the feedback, he explained that, "Now, instead of jumping in with humor in a stressful situation in order to lighten the mood, I pause and try to take the temperature a bit more." He concluded that the feedback "got me to reflect on how I am perceived more generally across situations."

Another example involves a senior female leader in information technology (and, yes, her gender is relevant to the example). For this leader, the penetrating message was the phrase "jumping to conclusions." As this leader recounts it, "I saw that in the comments, and my reaction was, 'Really? Am I really not listening?'"

Then, as with the leader in our last example, this leader began really reflecting on the feedback, and she concluded that, "Because this challenge was raised in my 360, I started seeing it in other areas of my life—in my social as well as my professional life." She went on to explain that, "The 'power woman' is a common thread among my friends, and I see that same trait in their behavior, as well."

This example, of course, could lead us to a deep and potentially worthwhile discussion of the challenges inherent in being a female leader. Anyone who has been in the field of leadership development for any substantial amount of time, regardless of gender, has no doubt had conversations with female leaders about how it can be tricky to be properly assertive without having others develop less than favorable (and frequently unfair) perceptions of the leader. While we completely acknowledge that this is an important issue, we are going to go in a different direction with this discussion—because the leader in our example did.

After some introspection, this leader said, "Now that I can see that behavior more clearly in others, I'm trying not to behave that way myself. Now it's like, 'I know how to fix this.'" In other words, regardless of any of the unique dynamics associated with being a female in a leadership role, this leader's response was to say, essentially, "Now that I am paying closer attention to this behavior in others, I realize I don't want to be seen that way." She focused on that issue over the course of several months, and she improved significantly, both in terms of her general effectiveness and in the specific area of openness to others' views.

To review, there are four factors that we found to be associated with feedback that leaders identified as penetrating messages. First, these messages were often communicated as short and even colloquial phrases. Second, they generally struck an emotional chord in the feedback recipient. Third, they sometimes involved seemingly conflicting feedback, with the key being that the leader earnestly sought to better understand the reason for the conflict and, more importantly, what could be done about it. And finally, the truly penetrating messages prompted real reflection on how the leader was coming across to others, inevitably resulting in the conclusion, "I'm not OK with that perception of me." Just as was the case with one of the authors of this book when told by his physician that his lifestyle could best be described as "sedentary."

The Coach as Messenger

As noted earlier, the penetrating messages that our most improved leaders cited may have come from a manager, a peers, a direct report, or even a leadership coach. As we reflected on this, we realized that in some of our more successful coaching engagements over the years, we as coaches often deliberately and strategically used what we hoped would be penetrating messages.

Consistent with the research cited throughout this book, our experience suggests that penetrating messages are a key component of improvement because an underlying emotion often drives behavioral change. Boldness and emotionality often transform a lackluster statement into a penetrating message. As noted earlier in this chapter, when leaders receive penetrating messages, they often have a strong emotional reaction emanating from the gap between the intent versus the impact of their behavior. We would also add a caveat to this, though. Penetrating messages can have a positive or negative impact, and thus, this must be considered as penetrating messages are delivered.

When we have considered the specific ways in which we as coaches have delivered penetrating messages over the years, two specific ways come to mind. Sometimes, we synthesize the messages about a leader into a provocative headline (for example, "Some people frankly just don't trust you") in hopes that this may resonate as a penetrating message. At other times we probe our leaders to explore their reactions to feedback and highlight their emotional reactions to it (by saying, for example, "It seems as though you are concerned that some people don't trust you"). These approaches vary in terms of who is generating the penetrating message. However, in both instances, the goal is for the leader we are working with to personally connect with a penetrating message that focuses and motivates him or her going forward.

As we brainstormed examples of instances in which we sought to deliberately and strategically deliver penetrating messages, two examples came immediately to mind. In one coaching engagement, one of us was working with a leader who came across to some as "spinning" and "selling" his point of view. So, in the leader's feedback summary, the coach used the term "Spin Doctor" as a headline to describe the way this leader was coming across to others. In another engagement, the coach used to term "Intellectual Bully" to reflect the leader's tendency to want to appear intellectually superior to others in his interactions.

We believe each of these examples generally meets the criteria for a penetrating message that surfaced in our research (short phrase, emotionally laden, etc.). And we believe that in each case, the coaching engagement ended up being very successful, although these particular leaders were not part of the sample for the study that is the focus of this book.

Conversely, we have also seen many instances in which the leader we are working with drives the focus on the penetrating message. For example, one of the authors delivered a feedback report to a leader that contained two core development messages ("You do not listen well enough" and "You tend to lowball your sales forecasts and overemphasize the headwinds you and your team are facing"). Although the coach believed the feedback on listening was the more prominent and important message, the leader himself reported that the "lowballing" comment really stuck with him.

Some coaches shy away from delivering or highlighting penetrating messages because of their own discomfort. An example from a coaching engagement within a large pharmaceutical company illustrates the effect of a coach not delivering a penetrating message when he probably should have. In this example, there was feedback indicating that the leader was not trusted by a number of coworkers. The author softened the message, in large part because of his personal discomfort in conveying the message too bluntly. The end result of this approach was that the leader in question dismissed the gravity of his behavior and ultimately did not improve meaningfully, and in fact, he was let go during the organization's next downsizing. Ultimately, the feedback related to trust proved not to be a penetrating message, perhaps in part because the coach did not deliver the message directly enough.

From all of this, we conclude at least two things. First, one of the keys to significant improvement among leaders is often the communication of a penetrating message—a short phrase that is emotionally laden, which sometimes helps a leader work through conflicting feedback, but which almost invariably causes some introspection on the part of the leader. Second, the leaders themselves are the ones who ultimately decide what is penetrating.

Recommendations

For the Leader

- Have healthy follow-up conversations with one or more feedback providers in order to better understand the feedback and act constructively on it.
- Several days after reviewing a feedback report, ask yourself what short phrase or colloquialism sticks with you from your feedback report. Although there may be a lot of feedback in any given report, this particularly penetrating message very well may be the single most important area for you to focus on.
- Seek to explain as broad a swath of feedback as possible with your penetrating message (in other words, ask yourself, "What theme or central issue does this penetrating message address?").
- Push yourself out of your comfort zone in order to truly grow and develop as a leader by thinking of penetrating messages as powerful agents of change. In other words, when feeling defensive because of some stinging penetrating message, embrace this as a motivator.
- See the penetrating message as an opportunity to build your emotional intelligence by developing greater self- and other-awareness.
- Try to quickly transition from being bothered by the feedback to figuring out what to do about the feedback.

For the Organization

- Create a section in your action organization's plan template that includes a heading called "Penetrating Message" so that your leaders reflect on their penetrating messages and discuss them with their managers.
- Link penetrating messages to organizational values, and encourage leaders to make action-planning decisions based on values and culture.
- Examine the type of culture and norms that exist within your organization. Not only are leaders motivated by penetrating messages that bother them in relation to their views of themselves as individuals, but they often also want

to avoid being viewed as "violating" some valued aspect of the organizational culture or values.

For the Coach

- Sometimes, deliberately decide to be the one to actually communicate the penetrating message by synthesizing feedback messages into a provocative headline.
- Help the leader understand that "others' perceptions are their reality."
- Divine a penetrating message and deliver it with both care and conviction—but err on the side of being challenging in order to tap into the underlying emotional factors that will help the leader understand the importance of the issue.
- Consider using words that capture emotional impact, not just practical impact (e.g., "Your peers *despise* your political behavior" rather than "You act politically toward your peers and they don't like it").
- Explore leaders' emotional reactions to help them articulate the penetrating messages they are taking away from their feedback. Penetrating messages often cause us to feel defensive (because of the very fact that they are penetrating). While the natural tendency may be for the leader to "lick his or her wounds," encourage leaders to recognize that this emotion can help focus them moving forward.
- Utilize probing questions and reflection to help leaders identify their own penetrating messages.

CHAPTER SIX

Guiding Metaphor

A specific conversation with one of our most improved leaders heavily influenced the decision to write this book. This leader was going through one of the high-potential leadership development programs offered by our firm, and the conversation was the last between this leader and his leadership coach (who is one of the coauthors of this book) at the very end of the nine-month program.

During this conversation, the coach asked some questions about what the leader thought accounted for his significant improvement. At some point the leader said, "I just needed to learn to stop giving people the answers to the test." Of course, this leader was not *literally* giving people answers to some test. There *were* no answers to a test! There was no *test*!

After the leader had used the "test" metaphor two or three times during the conversation, the coach asked him to elaborate on what he meant by "not giving people answers to the test." His reply was essentially that his original 360-degree feedback indicated that his natural leadership style was simply to tell people what he thought they should do when confronted with some sort of problem or challenge. This made him come across, to some at least, as an overly directive leader.

This approach actually seemed to be working quite well for this leader, at least on one level. The leader was widely respected, as evidenced by his extremely good feedback. And, in fact, as of this writing he has been identified as the leading internal candidate to move into the most senior position in his function when his manager retires. But he knew that his approach was less than optimal. On one hand, he was smart and experienced and had strong integrity, so his answers to challenges faced within his organization tended to be very sound and well received.

On the other hand, his natural approach—giving people the answers to the test—tended not to foster the sort of critical thinking, problem-solving, and independence that he needed from those who reported to him (who themselves were in leadership roles). So he made this his central issue.

But, beyond that, he came up with a *metaphor* that represented what he needed to work on. And then, when he was interacting with a direct report (or anyone else, for that matter) regarding some business challenge, the metaphor would come back to him and help him remember what he was working on. We suspect that there were many times when he had the thought, "Wait, I need to be careful not to just give him/her the answers to the test." When this happened, he would then change his approach. For example, he would ask a good question (such as, "What do you think our options are?") instead of just providing whatever guidance came to mind.

In other words, by keeping this metaphor in mind day to day, he avoided always just "giving people the answers to the test." And after several months of working on this central issue, keeping this metaphor constantly in mind, his already excellent 360-degree feedback was even better—dramatically so.

The Nature of Metaphor

A metaphor can be defined as a figure of speech in which a word or phrase is applied to an object or action to which it is not literally applicable. In the example we just cited, "not giving people answers to the test" was a phrase that applied to an action (telling people what to do) when it was not literally applicable (since there was no *literal* test).

We found that many of our most improved leaders had some sort of key metaphor that represented their central issue and that was an easy and memorable point of reference. Such metaphors provided these leaders with a high degree of *guidance* about how to act in a more effective manner, and they did so in a way that was condensed and personally meaningful. Hence, we have chosen the phrase "guiding metaphor" to get at this insight.

While a leader's use of a metaphor may be conscious, we found that often it is subconscious, as the example at the beginning of this chapter illustrates. In that last conversation between the leader and his coach at the end of the leadership development program, the coach brought to the leader's attention that he had used the same metaphor ("giving people answers to the test") multiple times to explain why he thought his feedback had gotten so much better. And his reply was, "Yeah, I guess I did latch on to that metaphor in order to remind me not to fall into old patterns of behavior."

Sometimes, the metaphors cited by our most improved leaders represented a way of *thinking* about one's key area for development. For example, one of our leaders, when interviewed about reasons for his dramatic improvement, said, "Well, for starters, my key area for development was like a tumor on the arm sticking up a few inches." This was his way of saying that his area was big, noticeable, and something that needed to be addressed, if possible. And that's exactly what he did.

More often, though, the metaphor represented an actual area for development. Thus, we have concluded that the primary value of a guiding metaphor is that if leaders are able to keep the metaphor in mind throughout the entire development experience, it's a way of helping them to stay focused on what they are working on.

Finally, we found it noteworthy that the metaphors that our most improved leaders used were, in general, not particularly creative, and many were, in fact, well-worn phrases and even clichés. But they were, nonetheless, effective in helping the leader keep his or her eye on the ball (pun intended). For much of the remainder of this chapter, we will discuss some of the specific metaphors used by our most improved leaders to address common leadership challenges.

Metaphors and Common Leadership Challenges

One of the authors was at dinner a few years ago with his spouse and another couple—both in fairly senior leadership roles in their organizations. The conversation turned to what the work of a leadership development consultant is like. The author who was at that dinner expressed the opinion that, "It seems like there are about a half dozen issues that we keep seeing over and over," though the specifics are, of course, different for each leader, team, or organization. This comment really seemed to resonate with both of the senior leaders we were dining with.

Interestingly, when we considered the specific nature of the different guiding metaphors that our most improved leaders had come up with to help focus their improvement efforts, we noticed that each metaphor seemed to relate to one of those key challenges that we see leaders struggling with over and over. We will discuss a few examples in the pages that follow.

Micro-Managing (or Being "Too Far in the Weeds")

We have worked with literally tens of thousands of leaders over the years, often with the benefit of feedback via a 360-degree feedback process. If we had a dollar for every time we saw the word "micro-manager" in feedback reports, we would have—well, lots of dollars. And we don't think it's usually a term of endearment.

Put simply, one of the most common issues that the managers we coach and train struggle with is a perception that they tend to micro-manage. In other words, they are too hands-on and provide overly detailed directions on how to do things, often even with senior people. This tends to result in at least a couple of problems. First, it tends not to be a great use of the more senior leader's time, since senior leaders should be focused on things like vision and strategy. Second, it tends to hurt employee engagement and can keep an organization from retaining its top talent.

Since it's such a common leadership issue, it came as no surprise that this was an example of a guiding metaphor from among our most improved leaders. For instance, one of our most improved leaders, when asked what he had focused on over the course of his leadership development program, said, "I needed to get out of the weeds." Of course, this is not a particularly original metaphor. However, as noted earlier, in general we found that the key metaphors that people kept in mind in order to improve were generally not all that deep or clever. Nonetheless, they seemed to work.

This leader went on to explain that he "had this metaphor in mind throughout the program," and when asked what the metaphor meant to him, he said that one thing the program taught him was that, "I don't need to be involved in every aspect of a project, and I shouldn't be." He added that he "should be more focused on establishing a larger direction," and noted that "sometimes you end up in a management position because you are really good at 'doing,' and I was trying to continue doing that plus setting direction, etc., and it was helpful for me to realize that I don't need to understand how every little thing works." Then he stated once again, "It was all a matter of getting out of the weeds."

Lack of Direction (or "Not Having a Tight Enough Rein")

The flip side of micro-managing is providing too *little* direction to people who may lack sufficient ability and/or motivation to perform well with lots of autonomy. This, too, is something that we frequently see the leaders we coach and train struggling with. And this, too, was something that was addressed via metaphor in our research.

Perhaps the best example of a metaphor to help a leader address this area for improvement is one that was cited in the previous chapter (on penetrating messages), the metaphor of needing to "have a tighter rein over my team." When asked how she responded to that feedback, this leader said, "I made sure that in each one-on-one meeting, I was going through expectations, giving them feedback, and so on." In addition, this leader said she "started asking more pointed questions about, 'How is this going? What do you need from me?'" Finally, the leader said that her direct reports "responded very positively, got better at giving her updates" and that "they didn't take it as micro-managing."

Interestingly, the first metaphor cited above (getting out of the weeds) was not something that appeared in the leader's feedback; it was just his shorthand way of referring to the central issue that did show up in his feedback. On the other hand, the tighter rein metaphor *did* appear in our second leader's feedback, and she latched onto it. In her words, "I kept this metaphor in mind as I continued meeting with my direct reports" after receiving the feedback. Thus, we have found that sometimes the metaphor emerges directly from the feedback a leader receives, and at other times the leader (or the leadership coach) can utilize a metaphor that seems to naturally fit the themes of the feedback.

Assertiveness (or Having an "Iron Hand in a Velvet Glove")

In addition to overleading and underleading, another issue that we often find the leaders we serve struggling with is assertiveness. The way we often frame this issue for leaders is to ask them to think of assertiveness as resting on a continuum, with passive behavior on one end, aggressive behavior on the other end, and assertive behavior in the middle.

Passive behavior involves allowing others to look out for their rights and interests at the expense of one's own. Aggressive behavior involves looking out for one's own rights and interests at the expense of others'. Assertive behavior involves both respecting the legitimate rights and interests of others and also properly standing up for one's own rights and interests.

We find that many leaders we work with are seen as being too far to the right or the left point on that assertiveness continuum. They are perceived as focusing either too much or too little on their own needs and views. One of our most improved leaders got just such feedback. This leader's job, at least in part, was to ensure that his organization was adhering to complex regulations related to international commerce.

The problem this leader was facing was that people thought he was overly aggressive. If the relevant regulations in a given situation created problems for a colleague, the way he tended to come across to others was, "Look, this is the way it is, so deal with it."

The thing is—he was largely right. Frequently, the rules really *were* the rules, and if they created issues for people in other areas of the company, it was generally the case that there was not a lot that this leader could do about it. So the key, on one hand, was to figure out how to ensure compliance with relevant regulations, and on the other hand, to do so in such a way that people did not perceive his behavior as overly rigid or noncollegial.

During one conversation with his coach about this challenge, this leader said, "I guess it's like having an iron fist in a velvet glove." Now, we're not sure how often this metaphor gets used these days, but for people in their 50s (as was the case for both the leader and his coach), this metaphor was perfect.

In this leader's words, "The 'iron fist' is the regulations I need to deal with, and that I need to get others to deal with; those are hard and fast." At the same time, this leader concluded that, "I can't just throw it at somebody and say, 'that's the way it is—live with it.'" The velvet glove part of the metaphor, in other words, was the way in which he communicated that message.

So the question became: How can he communicate messages in a way that comes across as properly assertive, rather than overly aggressive? Once the leader got to the point at which the basic nature of the change he needed to make was clear, the specific behaviors he needed to adjust were not that complicated. It was a matter of really listening to people, making eye contact, reflecting back what he was hearing, letting people know he understood and appreciated their concerns, and taking time to explain why things needed to be done a certain way.

But these actions were all pretty tactical. The bigger picture was the idea of that iron fist in the velvet glove. In fact, as this leader put it, "That analogy often came to mind when I was interacting with people." And that's the beauty of the key metaphor—it amounts to a vivid image that captures the essence of what the leader is working on, and it allows the leader to keep his or her central issue front of mind.

Demonstrating Competence (or "Understanding the Nuts and Bolts")

There is an exercise that we have done countless times in our leadership development workshops. We ask a group of managers to think of "the most effective leader you have ever known," and then we ask them to list and then call out their responses to that question as we capture their responses on a flip chart or a white board. This simple exercise invariably leads to some very interesting insights.

One such insight is that there is rarely much, if anything, that the managers come up with related to technical competence. They don't tend to comment on the leader's intelligence, knowledge of the industry, or deep understanding of the company's products or services. Rather, they comment on things like communication skills, genuine concern for the welfare of employees, skill at coaching and inspiring others, and other such non-technical skills.

However, we have noticed through years of experience that there is an exception to the general rule that people tend to associate strong nontechnical skills with highly effective leadership. The exception, of course, is when a leader lacks at least a solid working knowledge of what his or her direct reports actually do. Such was the case with one of our most improved leaders.

When this leader was asked what he most remembered about the feedback he had gotten at the outset of his leadership development program, his response was, "Someone mentioned something about digging into details and sometimes not understanding the whole scope of the job of my direct reports." Then he added that his central issue was being better able to "understand the nuts and bolts" of what his people did.

Once again, we see the power of metaphor. There of course were no actual nuts, and there were no actual bolts. But there were details associated with people's jobs that they thought their leader did not adequately understand when he asked them to take on various duties. This leader said that feedback "really rang true" for him.

He said that now, when he delegates some responsibility to a direct report, he stops and asks himself, "What am I really asking this person to do?" Further, he revealed that, "Now I stop and think: What are all steps this person is going to have to take?" Sometimes he knows the answers to these questions, and sometimes he needs someone else (potentially the direct report in the situation) to help him better understand what is actually involved in performing a given duty. In other words, he tries to better understand the "nuts and bolts" of what his people do, so that he is more effective at assigning duties, creating deadlines, and holding people properly accountable. And, as a result, he is seen as a more competent leader—not to mention a more effective leader in general.

Providing Effective Feedback (or "Not Piling On")

One of our leaders got feedback at the outset of one of our leadership development programs that he had a style that came across as intimidating, and in particular that the people he managed often thought his feedback was less than helpful. Working on this style became this leader's central issue.

When his feedback several months later was significantly better, he explained that what he had been working on primarily was not "piling on." Asked to explain what specifically he had been doing differently, he said that now, when he started to give someone feedback, he was careful not to give feedback on one issue, followed by another, and then another. In fact, one thing he said he was more conscious of was the use of the phrase, "and another thing." When he heard himself using that specific phrase, it signaled to him that he was about to "pile on." The effect of this was that it was overwhelming to the person he was delivering feedback to. So, he concentrated on staying focused on a single issue when delivering feedback, rather than piling on, and he became much more effective over time.

Communication Effectiveness (or "Talking So They Can Take Notes")

Perhaps the single most common area for improvement we see among the leaders we work with is some version of communication effectiveness. This, of course, can refer to many different skills. Two of our most improved leaders identified variations of communication effectiveness as their central issues, and each came up with a key metaphor to help foster improvement.

The first of these leaders identified "clear communication" as his central issue. When he was interviewed about the significant strides he had made in this area, based on a second round of 360-degree feedback, he recounted something that he had discussed with his coach during the leadership development program.

"I had a professor at [college]," he explained, and "I wanted to speak like he did during his classes." When asked to describe what made that professor an effective communicator, this leader said, "When he presented his topic for the day, he spoke really concisely, so that I could take notes on everything he said." In addition, this leader said that, "When he [the professor] got to something that was important, he would emphasize or repeat his point."

The metaphor in this example was, essentially, "I am like the professor, and the people I'm communicating with are like my students." This leader latched on to a particular aspect of his former professor's style that was vivid and something the leader could emulate. In the leader's words, "I got the idea that I should speak so clearly that people can take notes." The leader added that this image (people attempting to take notes during his presentations) was something that "came back to me whenever I was presenting in public or leading a conference call."

In fact, something interesting happened with this particular leader. During the interview for this study, he said, "Even this morning when I led our big national conference call, I told myself, 'Keep it slow so that people can take notes.'" That's the idea behind the key metaphor—it creates a mental picture that helps the leader focus on what he or she is working on.

Leadership Presence (or "Practicing as If I'm Going to Sing")

Another of our most improved leaders also focused on communication effectiveness, but his specific area for improvement was a little different. This leader was in a role in which he was increasingly expected to make presentations, and the perception was that he needed to work on his "leadership presence." As he reflected on his feedback, it occurred to him that there was something from his personal experience he could draw on to help him to be more effective when giving presentations in the corporate setting.

This leader was a singer who regularly performed in front of reasonably large groups. And the light bulb that went on for this leader was that he would never think of performing as a singer without extensive preparation—knowing the lyrics to the songs he would be singing inside and out, knowing in advance what sort of phrasing he wanted to use as a vocalist, and so on.

As this leader put it, "I am a singer, and the metaphor was to practice as if I'm going to sing in front of a group." This leader elaborated, saying, "I would never sing in front of a group without preparing, so I should prepare the same way when presenting—that metaphor was huge." In fact, during this leader's interview, he noted that he had just recently copresented with one of his direct reports, and he had insisted that the two of them rehearse as if it were a performance. The presentation went very well, he said, and his direct report expressed gratitude that the leader had him prepare so extensively.

Self-Management (or "Waiting to Open the Soda Can")

Sometimes, guiding metaphors also provide a visual representation that speaks to leaders. One leader identified the following metaphor to help increase composure and timing: "When I get angry, it's like shaking and then immediately opening a soda can." The work with this leader involved "waiting longer to open the soda can." This memorable, visual representation of the leader's central issue translated his idea (trying to be better at self-management with his team) into action (developing behavioral strategies, like waiting until the next day to respond to colleagues who had frustrated him).

It's worth noting that the last few insights we have covered (central issue, penetrating message, and guiding metaphor) all impact the way a leader thinks and even feels about what he or she is working on. That is, these insights explain how leaders gain focus, become motivated to change, and keep key issues front of mind. In the next chapter, we transition from focusing on insights that pertain to one's internal thought processes to an insight that has more to do with the relational aspect of behavior change.

Recommendations

For the Leader

- Create a guiding metaphor that is relevant to your central issue and that is memorable.
- Keep your guiding metaphor in mind, especially in situations in which you expect that your developmental issues may come up (that is, visualize your metaphor ahead of time).
- Think through the good implications of your metaphor, and the bad implications if the metaphor becomes more of a caricature.
- Consider what replacement metaphor you would like to be known for.

For the Organization

- Reflect on the guiding metaphors that may exist across the company; many organizations have historical events, dynamics, and cultural norms that have created organizational-level metaphors that can be leveraged on an individual basis.
- Encourage senior leaders to share their guiding metaphors as an act of normalizing the idea that leaders can benefit from creating guiding metaphors to help them stay focused on their developmental areas.
- Consider which metaphors *work* within your company's culture (movie references, sports, history, etc.), and encourage those.
- Reinforce metaphorical concepts in other ways, so that individual metaphors are not out of place in your organizational culture.

For the Coach

- Reflect on your knowledge of metaphors in general; seek to increase your repertoire of good, business-relevant metaphors so that pulling them out at the right moment comes easily to you.
- Look for metaphors in a leader's feedback, draw the leader's attention to them, and help the leader translate a key metaphor into one or more action steps.

- Listen for metaphors used by the leader during coaching conversations, draw attention to them, and help translate them into productive action.
- Think about metaphors that you as the coach can use in order to really get the leader's attention and influence him or her toward productive action in a specific area; in some cases you may have to try out one or two metaphors with a particular leader before one sticks.
- Have multiple categories of metaphors to pull from as examples when helping someone craft his or her own.
- Be prepared to run a reality check on a person's metaphor to make sure it both makes practical sense and does not perpetuate the issue the leader is working on.

CHAPTER SEVEN

Critical Conversations

Over the years, we have come to conclude that one of the biggest benefits of the sort of leadership development program that a consulting firm like ours offers is this: *It creates opportunities for critical conversations that might not otherwise happen.* This belief was validated by our interviews with our most improved leaders. Time and again these leaders indicated that they had engaged in a series of provocative discussions that caused them to engage with others on a series of important topics that likely would not have been bridged had they not been participating in the leadership development program to begin with.

The skeptic might question the significance of this finding, believing that engaging in conversation in the workplace is about as ubiquitous as breathing. However, the nature of the discussions these individuals engaged in differentiated these conversations from typical workplace conversations. They were engaging in meaningful, critical conversations that served as a pivot point for them in leading differently.

Let us illustrate with what we have found to be a fairly typical situation. A leadership coach is having a conversation with a leader that he or she is working with. The leader is describing some situation that really should be addressed with his or her boss, a peer, or a direct report. The coach asks, "So have you talked with this person about this?" It may seem obvious that there needs to be some sort of interaction between the leader and the person he or she has the issue with, but it's amazing how often we learn that leaders simply aren't having conversations that they really should be having on the job.

We call such interactions "critical conversations," and they can serve various functions, such as closing the feedback loop, building professional relationships, addressing important issues that have been festering,

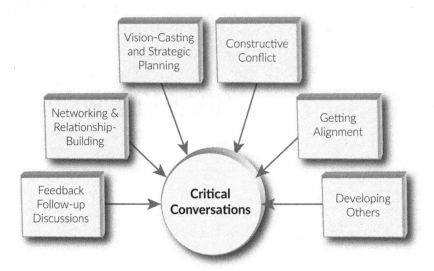

Figure 7.1

increasing clarity regarding goals and expectations, and many others. In short, they are conversations that probably should have been happening as a matter of course, but have not been, for whatever reason.

It became extremely clear to us in reviewing our data that when leaders saw the leadership development experience as a trigger or an opportunity to converse with others in ways that were quite different from how they typically communicated with coworkers, it had a dramatic impact on their working relationships and on how they were perceived by others. Put differently, their leadership development experience provided them with a reason or vehicle to have healthy, constructive, candid conversations on the job.

We believe that part of the beauty of a well-designed leadership development program is that it virtually *requires* that people interact in ways that may be at least somewhat outside the norm for them. The range of types of critical conversations reported on by our most improved leaders is highlighted in Figure 7.1, and we will review each of these in turn throughout the remainder of the chapter.

Feedback Follow-up Discussions

For many years we have encouraged the leaders we work with, at least those who have received some sort of feedback as part of the leadership development process, to follow a simple, three-step follow-up process: (1) develop an action plan; (2) discuss the action plan with those who provided the feedback; (3) engage in ongoing follow-up. These follow-up discussions represent one form of critical conversations that all of our most improved leaders engaged in.

Years ago, widely respected leadership coach Marshall Goldsmith published research indicating that leaders who were seen by coworkers as having engaged in little or no follow-up had slightly greater than 50–50 odds of being seen as more effective months later. Leaders who were seen as having engaged in frequent follow-up, on the other hand, had greater than 90–10 odds of being seen as more effective months later.[1]

Goldsmith's groundbreaking research changed the way we do leadership development. Before that, the focus of leadership development efforts tended to be on the actual intervention (for example, the insights and intentions generated through participation in a leadership training program or a coaching engagement). From that point on, though, most of us in the field of leadership development realized that the nature and extent of the leader's *follow-up* after participation in whatever the intervention was (the training program, the 360-degree feedback process, and so on) was at least as important to changing perceptions of effectiveness as participation in the intervention itself.

Initial Follow-up

We have taken to using the term "initial follow-up" to refer to initial conversations people have with their coworkers in order to inform others of what they are working on and to share their action plans. "Ongoing follow-up," on the other hand, refers to periodic conversations that happen over time between the leader and his or her coworkers, for the purpose of reminding people what the leader is working on and soliciting feedback on how the leader is doing on the development area(s) he or she has identified.

Actually, as we waded into our interview data, we realized we needed to take one step back when it came to initial follow-up, as the very first critical conversation a leader typically has as a part of a leadership development program, at least the kind our firm offers, is not with his or her manager, direct reports, or peers—it's with his or her leadership coach. And one thing we noticed about our most improved leaders is that the initial conversation with one's coach had the potential to be the first of numerous critical conversations.

As one leader put it, "For me, the critical conversation was the initial conversation with my leadership coach." This person elaborated, stating that, "It was helpful going through my results and getting the insight my coach provided." Coaches add value in a variety of ways in these feedback-debriefing discussions. For example, it is our experience that coaches assist by identifying higher-order themes or patterns in the data; asking effective questions to get at the root causes of perceptions others have of the leader; helping the leader overcome resistance, defensiveness, and other emotions that may inhibit constructive responses; and even helping the leader identify useful action steps that can be taken to address one's feedback.

One particular type of insight a leadership coach can provide is guidance regarding how to translate all of the messages a leader gets from his or her feedback into a sound action plan. As one leader put it, "I remember when my coach and I got together and we talked about my plan—there were a couple things my coach pointed out that were like an 'aha.'" This leader continued, saying that, "I think I was trying to over-engineer my plan, and my coach got me to think about how to incorporate action steps into my routine instead of making my action plan some huge project." This leader concluded that, "The focus that my coach provided helped."

Once a leader has had that initial critical conversation with his or her leadership coach, we think—and our research supports—that it is important for the leader to have several more critical conversations regarding his or her feedback and action plan.

Generally, we strongly encourage any leader we are working with that the next person to have a conversation with is his or her immediate manager. We recommend having this second critical conversation with one's manager because we believe it is important for the leader to align his or her area(s) of focus and action steps with the manager's priorities for him or her. And, indeed, a number of our most improved leaders indicated that the conversations they had with their managers were important and helpful.

One of our leaders, for example, stated that, "My manager had some good ideas about getting more visibility." In fact, this comment illustrates one of the primary purposes of having a critical conversation with one's manager before sharing one's plan with a broader audience—it gives the manager an opportunity to offer suggestions on the leader's initial action plan. In this example, the leader we were working with was able to adjust her action plan, based on her manager's feedback, before sharing the plan with direct reports or peers. This ensured that the leader did not publicly commit to a course of action that her manager thought was incomplete, or worse, that her manager had concerns with.

Over the course of our careers in the field of leadership development, we have each had experiences when the general feedback would suggest that an individual should take action in a particular area that was inconsistent with, or antithetical to, what the individual's manager expected. For example, one of the authors worked with a leader who was perceived by peers and direct reports as leading change in an insensitive and even disrespectful manner. If the leader were simply to act on the basis of his feedback, he might decide that he should soften his style and adopt a more collaborative approach. However, upon discussing the situation with his manager, the leader learned that the expectation from above was to continue pushing hard for change, regardless of any hurt feelings. In fact, the individual was told that if he "took his foot off the gas, his bonus would suffer." This example illustrates the importance of aligning one's action plan with one's manager prior to speaking with other stakeholders.

The next critical conversation our most improved leaders had tended to be reviewing their feedback findings and action plan with their other feedback providers (direct reports, peers, and other critical stakeholders). Some leaders, for example, prefer to initially follow-up in writing with their feedback providers. One of our leaders stated, "I sent out an e-mail to everybody who took the 360 survey, and I followed a template that my leadership coach provided." This leader further explained that, "In the e-mail I thanked them and told them what would happen next as a part of the process." As alluded to by this leader, we have begun offering leaders an actual template that they can use as a starting place for this sort of written follow-up, because this is clearly an efficient and, for many leaders, comfortable way of initially following up.

Beyond potentially sending out an initial follow-up e-mail, of course, we also encourage leaders to engage in some person-to-person follow-up. In fact, the leader just mentioned who started with a "to all" e-mail said that, "I then followed up with direct reports both in a team and in a one-on-one setting." This leader added that, "I got some good nuggets from people regarding their feedback and recommended actions." This comment raises the question: Is it best to discuss one's feedback and share one's action plan in a one-on-one or in a group setting? From our perspective, the answer is, "Yes." In other words, if possible—do both. However, as with the question of whether to initially disclose a bit about one's feedback and share one's action plan in writing, we have learned that leadership development is not a one-size-fits-all kind of thing, so we try to help each leader we work with come up with an approach that will work well for that leader.

For example, the leader just alluded to found it helpful to meet with direct reports initially as a group and then one on one. On the other hand, another of our leaders preferred only one-on-one discussions, saying, "I had individual discussions with peers about what I had heard in general, and also about the course—what I liked and what I was learning." Yet another leader met with his direct reports only in a group setting, saying, "I had one massive meeting that included everybody in my subordinate group. I read some of the results, what my scores were, and what I needed to work on."

In short, we believe that it is important to have one or more critical conversations with one's feedback providers, although the specific approach—one on one, group, or both—should be tailored to a given leader's situation and preferences. Again, a skilled leadership coach can work with a leader to develop a game plan that will be effective for that leader.

Another question that often comes up in our work with leaders going through a feedback and development process is: "Should I share what I have learned from my feedback even with feedback providers who did not provide feedback?" In other words, it is often the case that not all of one's direct reports or other stakeholders provided feedback through whatever the feedback-gathering process was. This could be for one of at least three reasons: The leader did not request feedback from all critical stakeholders; not all critical stakeholders chose to provide feedback; or one or more critical stakeholders joined the team after the feedback had already been gathered.

The question of sharing is a fair one, since there could be some awkwardness around a leader sharing insights from his or her feedback when one or more critical stakeholders may be thinking, "Feedback? What feedback?" While we acknowledge this potential awkwardness, we still think it's a good idea for a leader to engage in this sort of initial follow-up with all critical stakeholders. One of our most improved leaders illustrated how this can work, explaining that, "With my direct reports, I had a more general discussion; then, for people who did provide feedback, I included something about my feedback and action plan in our weekly 1:1 staff meetings." In other words, this leader took a more general approach with the entire team of direct reports and then discussed her feedback and action plan more specifically with those who were actually among the feedback providers.

All of this, of course, prompts the question: Exactly *why* is it so important to have these sorts of initial conversations? We have long believed that these initial conversations are critical to the improvement process, and we have long speculated about why such conversations are so important. Our research, however, provided data to support our claims about the *reasons* for having these initial, critical conversations. There are many such reasons, but four in particular clearly surfaced in our research.

First, it is simply a way of letting people know what the leader has learned from the feedback and, more importantly, what he or she plans to do differently. As one leader put it, "After I developed my plan, I had conversations with my direct reports and peers and told them what I was doing and why I was doing it—that was step one in implementing the plan." In other words, what we don't want to have happen is for people to provide a leader with feedback and then to feel like the feedback just disappeared into the old organizational black hole. Having this sort of initial conversation about one's feedback is a way of simply closing the loop with those who provided the feedback.

A second reason for having one or more key initial conversations with people is that it prepares people for the changes that the leader will be making. When we are working with a group of leaders in a leadership development program, we will often make the point that as soon as a leader has received developmental feedback, he or she is in a quandary. On one hand, if the leader doesn't go back on the job and somehow act differently, he or she can't possibly improve. In other words, people can't see what a leader has *learned;* they can only see what a leader *does.* On the other hand, if a leader does go back and act differently, people may think it's strange. The solution? Prepare people for the change. As one leader articulated it, "The changes I was making may have been awkward for others, but change without any conversation prior to it may have felt even *more* awkward."

Yet another reason for the importance of these initial conversations, based on our research, is that they demonstrate to others that the leader is indeed taking his or her development as a leader seriously. One leader illustrated this idea by saying, "I had a conversation with my direct reports and I think that was pretty meaningful because they appreciated understanding how seriously I was taking the leadership development process, and they were interested in how I was using the feedback to make improvements." Similarly, another of our most improved leaders said that when he shared a bit about his feedback and action plan with his team, "It was kind of an emotional moment for me," and that, "Them seeing me struggle through that gave them a sense of, 'Well, this guy is taking this seriously.'"

Put simply, when people see a leader really taking feedback to heart and striving to improve, that action alone seems to create more favorable impressions of the leader. Indeed, we find it noteworthy that an author we cited extensively earlier in this book, Jim Collins, found that one of the qualities that distinguished leaders who had taken their organizations from good to great was "personal humility."[2] And when a leader is willing to say to his or her coworkers, "Here is what I have learned about myself and here is what I plan to do more effectively going forward," that humble message seems to be well received by others.

Finally, this sort of initial conversation is an opportunity for the leader to let people know that he or she will be soliciting ongoing feedback from coworkers in the weeks and months ahead, in order to ensure that the leader is indeed improving. One of our leaders illustrated this, saying, "I explained what I had heard from my feedback, and I let them know that I would be asking for their feedback periodically." Of course, once a leader has indicated that he or she will be periodically asking for such feedback, it is important that the leader actually do so.

There is an important caveat to the recommendation to engage in initial follow-up discussions. Feedback, particularly at first, can trigger a wide range of emotions. In fact, people often go through a predictable emotional response cycle we refer to as SARAH.

Surprise
Anger
Resistance
Acceptance
Help

When people receive pointed developmental feedback, their initial reaction is often one of surprise. This surprise sometimes leads to anger: Anger that someone would think this about the leader; anger that nobody had ever raised the issue more directly; anger that people are ascribing the behavior to a less-than-noble motivation. The anger often triggers resistance to the message. Resistance can take the form of defensiveness, justification, and just generally debating the perceptions of others. The bottom line regarding resistance, however, is that individuals are not open to the message conveyed via feedback.

This trio of emotions (surprise, anger, and resistance) inhibits meaningful progress in developmental areas. However, as time passes, most of the leaders we've worked with become less emotionally charged about the feedback they've received. In fact, the vast majority come to accept that there is at least some truth to even their more critical feedback (for example, we often hear things along the lines of, "While I may not agree with the entire scope of the feedback I've been provided, I do see some truth in some situations to the message I've received"). Only when a leader is at least generally accepting of the feedback is he or she likely to seek help or take meaningful action to address the feedback.

The caveat regarding initial follow-up discussions is that a leader must be sure that he or she is not going to behave in a manner that exacerbates the situation or further entrenches the perceptions that others hold of them.

To be sure, being defensive, overly justifying one's prior actions, trying to deduce who said what in a confidential feedback report, only focusing on the negative feedback one receives, and making jokes about one's feedback are understandable (initial) reactions to feedback. However, these reactions do more harm than good and certainly don't suggest to feedback providers that a leader is likely to make substantive changes. As such, we tend to encourage people to hold off on engaging in initial follow-up discussions until they have moved through some of the early stages of the SARAH model and are prepared to demonstrate a mature, accountable, and solution-oriented demeanor in response to feedback.

Ongoing Follow-up

The other type of follow-up we have long encouraged leaders to engage in is ongoing follow-up, and our research indicates that this, too, is an important type of conversation for a leader to be having with his or her coworkers after some sort of leadership development experience. These ongoing discussions about one's development efforts fall under our heading of "critical conversations" because our research suggests that such conversations helped our most improved leaders to make ongoing changes in their behavior that, in turn, resulted in more favorable perceptions of the leaders' effectiveness.

Maybe these ongoing conversations were so critical because they reinforced the actions a leader was already taking ("I've seen real improvement in that area—thanks!"). Alternatively, perhaps they were so valuable because they allowed the leader to realize that the actions he or she was taking weren't having sufficient impact ("Hey, I'm afraid you just did that thing you said you weren't going to do anymore"). Yet another possible explanation for the importance of these discussions is that they highlighted to feedback providers and other organizational stakeholders the commitment leaders had to enhancing their effectiveness ("Wow, I'm impressed with how diligently you're approaching your development"). All of these likely help explain why ongoing follow-up represents a type of critical conversation.

Perhaps not surprisingly, the target audience for these follow-up conversations is the same group of people with whom leaders should have had their initial conversations (for example, coaches, managers, direct reports, peers, and other important stakeholders). For starters, our research revealed that the regular conversations with an external leadership coach as part of structured leadership development programs are indeed seen as helpful. As one of our most improved leaders said, "My conversations with my leadership coach were really good," adding that, "As an objective third party, my coach provided feedback as he saw it, and his feedback was always constructive and honest."

We found that our most improved leaders generally had rich, ongoing conversations with their managers about their improvement efforts, as well. In some cases, the leaders going through the development process initiated these conversations. For example, one leader explained that, "I built discussions about my action plan into my one-on-one meetings with my manager; we just made it part of our process." In other cases, it was the manager who took the initiative, as the following case illustrates: "My boss started bringing up my action plan up in each of our one-on-one meetings. So, I made it a point to bring my plan to each meeting with my manager."

This idea of just "making it part of the process," regardless of who initiates the ongoing conversations, was a common theme regarding ongoing follow-up that ran through a number of comments from our interviews. In each example just cited, for instance, it wasn't as though the leader we were working with and his or her manager scheduled lots of additional meetings. Rather, they said, "We already have regular one-on-one meetings—let's just build ongoing discussion related to the leader's feedback and action plan into those regular conversations." One way or another, though, our research suggests that leaders who improve significantly tend to talk regularly about what they are working on with their managers.

Our most improved leaders generally also had consistent follow-up conversations with their other feedback providers. In some cases, the approach was similar to that of the two leaders mentioned above—they simply made these conversations a part of their normal process, only they did it with a broader set of stakeholders. As one leader explained, "I was already having weekly one-on-one meetings with my direct reports, and after getting my feedback I just made discussion of my action plan an agenda item, and I always brought my plan to these meetings."

These leaders stressed the importance of regularly asking feedback providers for feedback on how they were doing relative to their action plans. For example, one of our most improved leaders shared an example that illustrates how this might actually work. This leader said, "With direct reports, I would ask them if my action steps were resonating, and if what I was trying to do differently was helpful." In this leader's case, part of her action plan involved improving her communication with her staff by ensuring that when she forwarded e-mails from her higher-ups, she also included some of her own color commentary. The goal was just to help her direct reports better understand the context and implications of messages coming from executive leadership.

Importantly, this leader stressed to her team that she was committed to really following through on this, and she said, "I asked them to call me out on it if I was not following through, which helped keep me honest." Interestingly, though, she noted that, "They didn't really have to do that, because I did follow through." In other words, this leader created some accountability for herself, and it worked—she really did follow through on her commitment to her team.

Consistent with a point we made regarding *initial* critical conversations, we think it's important for leaders to come up with an approach to these *ongoing* critical conversations that really works for them. For example, one of our most improved leaders expressed reluctance to request ongoing feedback with direct reports in general, for various reasons. However, this leader explained that, "I focused most on the team members I have a rich history with, and asked them to be candid with me on things I was working on." As with other examples, this leader stated that, "Early on they were not comfortable with this, and actually asked if they could e-mail their feedback to me."

All of this suggests that, for whatever reason, there was a bit more caution in this example regarding who might be willing to provide feedback, and even how they might go about providing it. This leader continued, somewhat humorously, "I never got the e-mails, but they did eventually break down and give me some feedback in person." It appears that this leader managed to find a way to deal with some sensitivity regarding people providing ongoing feedback, and everything ended up working out well.

In summary, our research provided support for two bits of counsel regarding following up on feedback that we have long provided to the leaders we work with. First, after getting developmental feedback, have some initial conversations with coworkers to let them know what you've learned and what you'll be working on. Second, have some ongoing conversations with coworkers to remind them what you are working on and find out whether they believe you are making progress. Frankly, we would have been surprised if we had not found support for these practices, in part just because they make so much sense.

Follow-up as the Gateway to Critical Conversations

In many cases, the sorts of follow up interactions we have described so far in this chapter *are* the critical conversations. The leader we are working with needs to be receiving feedback from his or her manager, and talking about his or her action plan during regular one-on-one meetings is the opportunity to do to. Or the leader we are working with needs to be making expectations of his or her direct reports clearer, and their one-on-one meetings provide the opportunity to do so. You get the idea.

But in other cases, these sorts of interactions related to initial and ongoing follow-up are really just the starting place for what these leaders really need to be talking about with their coworkers. In other words, these follow-up interactions can, and based on our research often did, serve as the *gateway* to critical conversations that really needed to be happening, based on the feedback received by the leader. Some of the common types of critical conversations our most improved leaders reported engaging in based upon the feedback they received included:

- Networking and Relationship-Building
- Vision-Casting and Strategic Planning
- Constructive Conflict
- Getting Alignment
- Developing Others

Given that most of the leaders in our sample were participants in high-potential leader development programs, this is an instructive list of critical conversations that the leaders we were working with apparently were not otherwise engaging in—at least not to the extent they needed to. What strikes us most about this list is that these are not exactly remedial topics. Rather, they represent a number of key skills one must excel at in order to succeed at more senior levels of management.

They also represent the sorts of topics that can get swept under the rug in today's go-go-go, execution-oriented business world. As such, these can be considered topics of focus for already successful leaders who want to position themselves for positions of greater responsibility. They can be seen as representing a need for leaders to broaden one's reach throughout an organization, and we will address each in turn.

Networking and Relationship-Building

One of the most common areas for development identified by the leaders we work with is some variation of networking or relationship-building. Especially in this era of matrix organizational structures and cross-functional collaboration, it's critical for leaders to have strong relationships across their organizations. However, in our experience, there are at least two reasons why this does not happen as a matter of course as often as it should.

One reason is that this sort of networking or relationship-building just doesn't bubble up as a big enough priority for many leaders. It's the proverbial high-importance but low-urgency to-do item. Why carve out time to have coffee with a leader from another area of the organization, with no particular agenda, when there are several urgent and important issues staring the leader directly in the face?

Another reason is simply that there is often no natural opening for one leader to approach another simply to build the relationship. How often, for example, do any of us have a meeting notice in our calendar that says, "Networking with Jane Doe," or "Relationship-Building with John Doe"?

In our view, part of the beauty of a well-crafted leadership development program is that it addresses both of these factors. First, feedback that a given leader needs to improve in this area might create some urgency that previously did not exist for that leader. And second, the feedback follow-up process creates a very natural opening for the leader to approach colleagues or even more senior leaders to have coffee (or whatever) when the leader may not be so bold as to do this under other circumstances.

Two of our most improved leaders exemplify this idea beautifully. One had identified internal networking as an area for development in his action plan, and one of his action steps was that he created a list of a half dozen peers within the organization with whom he felt he needed to build some bridges. So, he scheduled a series of networking meetings with these peers—over lunch or coffee, and with no particular agenda. He stated, "Of the handful of leaders I chose for the networking meetings, most of them were people I had never worked with, and my action plan opened the door to those relationships."

Another leader whose experience exemplifies this insight also included in her action plan some networking conversations. In this leader's case, there was more emphasis on meeting with even more senior executives (a common theme for participants in a high-potential program, who are likely very effective in their current roles, but need enhanced exposure in order to be positioned for expanded roles). This leader noted that, "Among other things, these [follow-up] meetings allowed me to share some things about my background with senior people that I might not otherwise have been able to do that with." In fact, this leader went on to reveal that, "One of my follow-up conversations was with a senior leader who became a mentor."

Think about that. A good mentor can change the whole trajectory of one's career, and in this case, if the leader had not had that executive on her networking conversations list as a part of her action plan, the critical conversation that led to the mentoring relationship may never have taken place.

In short, these sorts of networking conversations are likely to seem to both parties to be more organic and less awkward, since it's not solely about the leader's feedback, action plan, and follow-up efforts. Framing a networking conversation in the context of one's feedback and then focusing on better understanding one another's areas of responsibility and hopes/concerns is likely a less clunky conversation than saying, "I'm working on X and I'd like to get your feedback on how I'm doing."

Vision-Casting and Strategic Planning

Another common area for development among the leaders we work with is being more visionary and/or strategic. This makes sense, in that most thought leaders in the field of leadership agree that something along the lines of casting a vision, setting a direction, and/or being strategic is part of the essence of what it means to be a leader.

In some cases, particularly gifted visionaries like Steve Jobs seem blessed with some capacity that allows them to seemingly see into the future and leverage huge organizations in developing products and services that reshape whole industries. In our experience, vision-casting and strategic planning is ideally more of a collaborative exercise, in which senior leaders may have some conviction about the direction an organization needs to take, but there is also a realization that gaining alignment and commitment through two-way dialogue is at least as important as the vision or strategy itself.

That's where another type of critical conversation emanating from a leadership development process can once again be almost priceless. One of our most improved leaders illustrated this perfectly. This leader noted that, "My central issue was being a more strategic leader," adding that, "This included networking with colleagues across the organization." In these strategy discussions with key stakeholders, this leader focused on asking questions like, "How can we help support your goals and the strategic path for *your* area?"

By the end of the leadership development program, this person's collaborative approach to strategy resulted in him being tapped to lead a strategic planning effort for his entire division, and the effort was seen as a huge success, helping the organization to advance its strategy and elevating his profile as a strategic leader.

Interestingly, this leader also noted that his regular one-on-one meetings with his leadership coach were also very helpful as a way of preparing for his strategy discussions and meetings on the job. Specifically, he indicated that his coaching meetings prompted him to "think through the strategic planning efforts" he was leading, including "how to approach the meetings, and who to reach out to in order to get input and feedback on our strategic planning efforts." So, for this leader, there were two types of critical conversations that helped him grow as a strategic leader: Conversations with his coach in order to help him prepare for strategy discussions on the job, and then those very strategy discussions.

Vision-casting and strategic planning represent a type of critical conversation because these sorts of discussions enable a leader to influence the direction of the company. Whether by offering an insightful, heretofore undiscovered strategic direction or by collaboratively facilitating a group of stakeholders to a single, focused, and aligned direction, the leader engaging in vision-casting and strategic direction is stepping up to the challenge of influencing organizational direction in a way he or she otherwise might not have.

Constructive Conflict

Yet another common area for development identified by the leaders we work with is something along the lines of "conflict management." Of course, the term *conflict* often has a negative connotation, as if it's something to be avoided or resolved. In our view, conflict is unavoidable, healthy, and even critical in any organization—provided it's handled well.

Unfortunately, in our experience conflict is often not handled well by the leaders we work with. Many leaders either shy away from it entirely or engage in conflict in a way that just worsens the situation. Therefore, it is not uncommon in our work with leaders to spend time discussing interpersonal skills related to effective conflict management (such as establishing common ground, being constructive in advancing one's own point of view, truly seeking to understand the other person's point of view, and so on).

Of course, at some point these leaders need to actually engage with the people they have some sort of disagreement with, unless their conflict management strategy is to try to avoid the conflict indefinitely—generally not a sound strategy. And we believe that an effective leadership development process can create the context for healthy engagement. Constructive conflict represents a type of critical conversation because it provides a leader with an opportunity to advance the dialogue or to become "unstuck" in his or her relationship with another person.

As an example, one of our most improved leaders had gotten feedback, largely from peers, indicating that he tended to come across as if he were "debating" others instead of seeking to find mutually agreeable solutions.

Further, this leader was prone to doing this in certain forums that others thought were particularly inappropriate places and times for such debates.

As part of this leader's follow-up to his initial feedback, he said, "I had conversations with my peers and asked, 'From your perspective, how would you have handled these sorts of situations differently?'" He said that two of these peers (both of whom were friends as well as coworkers, incidentally) "told me that I just need to be aware that certain forums we are in together are not appropriate forums for debate." As this leader continued to focus on conflict management as his central issue, with a particular focus on better understanding when it was and was not appropriate to engage with others using his default conflict style, he improved dramatically.

Sometimes, a leadership coach can spur a leader to have a conversation with another person that the leader has been avoiding or with whom the coach believes there is likely to be a critical conversation. Such was the case with the following example.

This example involved a Human Resources (HR) leader who, after getting some "mixed" feedback from various stakeholders, was encouraged by his coach to go speak directly with the most senior business leader he supported in order to get additional clarity and alignment in relation to some of the feedback. The coach already anticipated that this conversation would allow the business leader to be more candid than he previously had been about his disappointment in the HR leader's poor support levels, which were largely the result of his inability to hold his HR team accountable. Further, the coach sensed that the leader being coached would want to hear that feedback and would be able to handle the direct message. In this case, the coach was able to create the circumstance for a critical conversation leading to constructive conflict when it may not have happened naturally. As the coach suspected, the business leader *did* highlight her concerns about the lack of accountability from the HR team, which allowed the issue to be put on the table and successfully addressed.

Getting Alignment

Closely related to the outcome of better managing conflict is the outcome of getting better alignment with one's peers in other areas of an organization. Two common causes of alignment issues are seemingly competing objectives between different parties and being so execution-oriented that leaders do not prioritize alignment discussions. Getting alignment represents a type of critical conversation in that engaging in such conversations enables teams, departments, and organizations to focus their efforts. One of our most improved leaders cited an example of just such a critical conversation with a group of peers.

This leader indicated that he and another important group seemed to be at cross-purposes with one another on an issue that kept coming up. The issue related to two seemingly competing goals: Getting products to clients as quickly as possible and being in compliance with certain guidelines for which the leader had accountability. Our leader was convinced of the rightness of his position (and, frankly, after having multiple conversations with him on the issue, his leadership coach was convinced, as well). Yet, this leader simply could not seem to influence key members of the other group to come around to his point of view.

Since the leader's feedback indicated that he came across as overly blunt and lacking in empathy, the leader decided to try having yet another conversation with members of the other group on this issue—but this time, using a different approach.

The leader called for a meeting, and started by saying that this time he really just wanted to listen until both he and his peers thought he really understood the other group's perspective on the matter. So that's what he did—he just listened. And then he reflected back to his peers what he thought he had heard, and they affirmed that he did indeed seem to understand the other group's position. Only at that point did the leader explain his position, and this time, he went farther than he ever had in walking his peers through the reasoning behind his position, instead of seeming to communicate the message, "That's just the way it is."

When recounting this conversation, our leader said he "finally saw the light bulb go on after having tried to make my point with this group many times before that." This critical conversation resulted in much better alignment between the two groups, and they arrived at a form of resolution that effectively met each group's needs. And the conversation may never have happened if not for the fact that our leader was genuinely interested in improving his approach, and was open to new ways of interacting with his colleagues.

Developing Others

Sometimes, a critical conversation involves a leader prioritizing skill-set development in others. Perhaps the leader is teaching someone else some things that the leader going through the development process is learning. Or perhaps the leader is simply taking time to deliver feedback and coaching to a direct report or someone else who the leader could choose to help develop. One leader illustrated with the following example.

This leader was working on being perceived as a more executive-level leader, and he had determined that the keys were to be more strategic and to project greater self-confidence. And he had a direct report who, in his view, had similar challenges.

As this leader recounted the story, he and this direct report were preparing to present to their internal partners in Corporate. He said, "I was kicking off with the 'why' and my direct report was then going to go into the 'how.'" He added that, "I encouraged him to do what I had been doing as a part of my own action plan, which is to prepare more for such presentations." So, they went through four or five practice sessions, with our leader asking his direct report, "What are you going to say? How are you going to say it?"

Our leader said that, "At the end of that day, my direct report looked at me and said, 'Thank you for making me practice.'" More importantly, our leader proudly exclaimed that, "Our audience was really blown away by how well our presentation went," and added that, "Now the direct report knows that he really needs to prepare." In the end, not only did this leader improve significantly, but he also used what he learned to interact with others—in this case, a direct report with similar challenges—to help others improve, as well.

This critical conversation led to the leader getting vulnerable in sharing his development goal, as well as his intention to develop his direct report by sharing knowledge he had received through the leadership development experience. The result was that the critical conversation positively impacted both the leader and his direct report. Such developmental discussions represented a common type of critical conversation that our most improved leaders engaged in.

Critical Conversations as a Way of Doing Business

There were other kinds of critical conversations that our most improved leaders said they were having, and having effectively, as a result of their initial efforts to follow-up on their feedback. Some took opportunities to address unhealthy team dynamics. Others found that their formal review discussions with their own managers and direct reports were much more effective. Still others realized that they needed to step up their efforts to meet with coworkers in person, rather than remotely.

Regardless of the specific purposes and forms that these critical conversations took, it was clear to us from our research that when leaders saw the leadership development experience as an opportunity to interact with others in ways that were quite different from how they typically communicated with coworkers, it had a dramatic impact on their working relationships and on how they were perceived by others.

These critical conversations required our most improved leaders to address sensitive topics, listen to the perspectives of others, and diversify the populations with whom they were interacting. Put differently, development doesn't occur in a vacuum. One must involve others and cultivate the ability to have healthy, constructive, candid conversations on the job—something that at least got a little closer to being just a way of doing business for our most improved leaders.

Recommendations

For the Leader

- Summarize your 360-degree feedback into themes regarding strengths and development opportunities, develop an action plan, and share this overview with feedback providers (direct reports, peers, your manager, and any other key stakeholders).
- Periodically touch base with feedback providers and other stakeholders to assess their perceptions of progress against your development goals.
- Utilize the 360-degree feedback or leadership development experience to have conversations about which you have either been procrastinating or haven't seen an effective method of initiating. Common topics of such conversations can include: Networking and Relationship-Building, Vision-Casting and Strategic Planning, Constructive Conflict, Getting Alignment, and Developing Others.
- Critical conversations involve effective listening and asserting. Ensure that you are appropriately balancing these two conversation elements.
- Spend time crafting the narrative—both the messages you've received and your intent to address them.
- In addition to an action plan, also create a communication plan that addresses communication channels, audience, frequency, level of detail, receiving reactions, etc.

For the Organization

- Build expectations for follow-up into your development experiences to ensure that participants are fully realizing the benefit that critical conversations offer.
- Set the expectation that follow-up on a leader's 360-degree feedback is a standard practice and have the most senior participants model this behavior.
- As a manager or peer of someone involved in a feedback or development process, proactively engage them about their experience—creating the "norm"

and expectation that they should be talking with you about their learning and goals coming out of the program.

For the Coach

- Set the expectation that following up on one's 360-degree feedback is a standard practice.

- Have the leader you are working with identify stakeholders with whom critical conversations would be meaningful. Explore any reticence the leader may have about initiating such conversations and encourage the leader to step out of his or her comfort zone. Karmen to Afua

- During coaching discussions, keep focusing on who else would benefit from hearing the sorts of topics you are discussing, and encourage the leader you are working with to engage in these discussions.

- Help the leader get skilled and comfortable by doing some "dry runs" of how these kinds of conversations might sound.

- Identify strategies for infusing critical conversations into the leader's standard business approach (by asking, for example, about what meetings or forums already exist that can be leveraged to initiate critical conversations).

- Be specific in terms of expectations for critical conversations (timing, audience, frequency, etc.).

CHAPTER EIGHT

Training Experience

It seems that *training* is often considered a four-letter word in the field of management consulting—even among many in the more specific field of leadership and organizational development. For some, training is seen as basic, generic, unsophisticated, and not very impactful.

While we acknowledge that leadership training can be all of those things, we also firmly believe that training that is based on genuine client needs, and that is well designed and well facilitated, can be an extremely impactful way of helping leaders to become more effective. And we believe this is especially the case when training is combined with other leadership development methods, such as 360-degree feedback, coaching, and action learning.

Indeed, our high-potential leadership development programs generally involve all of the elements just mentioned, and we have found that training sessions frequently result in realizations on the part of leaders (the proverbial "aha experience") that they may not experience any other way.

In our interviews with our *How Leaders Improve* sample, one thing we explored was whether there was a particular aspect of the training they went through as a part of their leadership development experience that had resulted in some sort of realization that actually paved the way for development. We found that there were, indeed—several of them, in fact.

Tone of Coaching and Workshops

Years ago, one of the authors had just the sort of aha experience we hope the leaders we work with will have. The author was serving as the facilitator and coach for a high-potential leader development program at a large technology company. The program involved about 10 people, and it was structured in a way that was similar to the high-potential programs that leaders being studied for this book participated in. Specifically, there was a feedback component, a training component, and a coaching component.

During one of the early one-on-one coaching sessions, one of these high-potential, high-performing leaders said to his coach: "I have to tell you, I'm not feeling the love." Startled, the coach asked the leader to elaborate, and he explained that, while a big deal had been made out of the fact that these particular leaders had been selected for this program because they were "high-potential and high-performing leaders," the program up until that point had been largely focused on what they were not doing very well. In other words, they got their feedback, and there was a cursory acknowledgment of their strengths, but then the focus of their action plans and the follow-up process was on their relative weaknesses.

This was right before all the research on strengths-based leadership development came out, and it was purely anecdotal. However, it had a huge impact on the coach, who changed his approach to leadership development from that point on. While many aspects of his approach remained the same (the approach to gathering feedback, many specific leadership skills taught in the workshop portion of the programs, etc.), there were two specific things that were changed.

First, much more attention was paid to leaders' strengths. This meant a number of things. There was more discussion of leaders' strengths, both in the coaching sessions and in the workshops, so that leaders had a better sense of exactly what they did especially well, why they did those things so well, and how they could better leverage those strengths. And action steps for building on strengths were much more deliberately, explicitly, and extensively built into leaders' action plans, so that they were not just trying to fix weaknesses, but also to make sure they were fully leveraging their strengths.

The second thing that was different was that more was done to ensure that both the coaching and workshop elements of these high-potential leader development programs had a celebratory, congratulatory, uplifting feeling to them. Never again did we want one of our clients' most promising leaders to feel like he was "not feeling the love" during one of our programs. So there was more of a concentrated effort to simply encourage the leader and boost his or her confidence in our coaching sessions, and more was done to create a positive, supportive climate in our workshops.

We were, therefore, encouraged that one of the themes from interviews with our most improved leaders was that they did find the training they participated in (including the coaching, the workshops, and the other aspects of our programs) to be positive experiences. This is not to say that the experiences were not rigorous and challenging—they certainly were. But for many of our most improved leaders, they were also inspiring. More specifically, there were at least two things about the positive dynamic of the whole leadership development experience that our most improved leaders highlighted.

First, some of our leaders noted how refreshing it was to be in a leadership development program with other high-potential, high-performing leaders. As one person put it, "It was great being there with people who were there for a reason, people who were enthusiastic participants." This leader continued that, "It was a group of people who were very interactive, they were all from [the same organization], and they all understood the company, which created a great environment for talking about things that were at times highly personal."

Similarly, another of our most improved leaders indicated that, "It meant a lot that I was in that room with nine other highly-thought-of leaders, and they also had areas to work on, which made me realize that everyone has issues—we are all just working on different things." In short, our research indicated that the *positive climate* created by being in a leadership development program with other particularly strong leaders was extremely beneficial.

This may seem obvious, but as any leadership development professional can attest, this theme from our research gets at the very heart of a key question we all have to wrestle with: Who exactly should enroll in our leadership development programs. This question gets answered in many different ways in our client organizations. Sometimes leadership training programs are mandatory for all leaders at specific levels within the organization or for all leaders within a given department.

Other times, an open enrollment approach is used, in which leaders can self-select into leadership development programs. And at still other times, leaders are selected based on some combination of potential and/or performance. And even then, there are variations; sometimes it's the high-performing leaders who are invited so that the company can invest in these leaders, and in other cases leaders who are struggling in a given area are asked to participate in a program that may help them address specific areas for improvement.

We suspect that, in large organizations at least, some combination of these methods will continue to be used, and we are not advocating adopting a single approach to identifying participants for a leadership development program. We *are,* however, suggesting that there is a positive dynamic that develops in programs involving high-potential, high-performing leaders, and that positive dynamic helps contribute to actual improvement.

Gifted : Talented !!)

A second factor that our most improved leaders associated with the positive tone of the whole experience was the encouraging nature of the 360-degree feedback itself. Of course, since these were high-potential, high-performing leaders, it is not surprising that they generally got good feedback to begin with, and some of them found that encouraging. As one leader said, "I think the 360 was tremendous, as far as confidence-building."

However, other leaders may have been less inclined to focus on their positive feedback if left to their own devices. Rather, they may have needed some encouragement to do so, and they found that encouragement in some of the content of the leadership development workshop, as well as the coaching.

One leader illustrated this, explaining that, "For me the original 360 feedback was key, and in particular identifying areas where I had spikes." While the term "spike" can be defined in different ways (a subject we delve into in more detail in Chapter 11), a simple definition is that it's a competency in which a leader scores in the top 10% as compared with his or her peers. This leader continued that, "That's something I take with me, and I have pride in the fact that I have several spikes, based on the research that was shared." And what was the impact? This leader said, "That made me feel good—proud that I do have those leadership attributes." Again, these sessions for our most improved leaders were not just about skill acquisition, they were about feeling encouraged and about developing greater self-confidence, as well.

Helpful Coaching

One of the authors spent much of his career as a leadership development consultant feeling quite uncomfortable with the coaching aspect of this profession. Quite simply, he didn't want to be anyone's guru. He didn't feel qualified for such a role. Who was he to be telling senior leaders with years of experience behind them and large organizations under them how to be more effective? Yet if one is in the field of leadership development, it is almost inevitable that one type of service the consultant is expected to provide is one-on-one coaching. And while this author's self-doubt has not completely disappeared over the years, it has been assuaged to a large extent by the fact that one need not be a guru in order to be an effective coach. Indeed, interviews with our most improved leaders found that the effectiveness of the coaching they received was mostly the result of a number of fairly simple practices engaged in by one's coach.

Interestingly, one thing that our leaders found effective about the coaching they received had absolutely nothing to do with the coach's skill, personality, approach, or anything like that. It was merely the fact that the coach represented an *outside point of view*. As one leader put it, "It was great to have that third party, objective person" to talk with on a regular basis. Another echoed this idea, saying, "How nice it is to have somebody who is impartial and not part of the organization giving you thoughts and ideas."

Another thing that the coaching aspect of the experience accomplished was that, quite simply, it created a level of *accountability* for our leaders. In most cases, our leadership development programs included monthly meetings with one's coach. In some cases, the meetings were in person, but many were by phone.

One objective for each coaching meeting was for the coach and the leader to discuss successes and challenges since the previous conversation. More specifically, the coach would generally ask, "What successes have you experienced in following through on your action plan since our last conversation?" Then, after some discussion about successes, the coach would ask, "What challenges have you encountered in seeking to follow through on your action plan?" That would then generally lead to some dialogue about what was working and should be continued and what was not working as well and should be revisited. And several leaders said that just having that sort of accountability helped them continue to follow through on their action plans.

This leads to another aspect of the coaching that our most improved leaders generally found helpful. When a leader had experienced challenges in following through on his or her action plan, the coach generally resisted the temptation to just start offering advice. Rather, the approach was to ask some questions to try to get the leader thinking about what he or she could be doing differently in order to address his or her challenges. In other words, the coach helped the leader come up with his or her own *action steps*.

And the feedback from our most improved leaders generally indicated that they found this approach helpful. One leader pointed out that, "For the most part, my coach helped me come up with my own action steps," and another stated that, "My coach generally didn't tell me what to do; he paved the way for me to see what would be beneficial," adding that, "I remember that vividly and found that very valuable." As with many of the things that drove improvement on the part of these leaders, the practice of simply asking good, open-ended questions is not rocket science. However, there is a discipline associated with it, and our leaders seemed to appreciate and find value in this approach.

Yet another way the coaching sessions contributed to our leaders' dramatic improvement was simply the *focus* that these conversations created. As we noted in Chapter 4, our most improved leaders were generally able to clear out all of the clutter in their feedback and focus on a central issue that represented, in essence, the most important lever to pull in order to improve. One of our leaders noted that, "I really liked the coaching sessions," adding that, "Our initial dialogue helped me to focus on that central issue, which was the key to success." Beyond that initial dialogue, the practice of meeting on a monthly basis and continuing to specifically refer to and discuss the leader's central issue ensured that the leader continued pulling that same lever.

So, simply being an outsider, having monthly meetings, and asking good questions were some of the keys to the coaching sessions seen as being helpful by our most improved leaders. Surely there must be more to it than that! Well, yes. There are a couple of other things that our leaders said they got out of the coaching that probably involved at least a bit more skill, courage, and finesse as a coach. One such facet of effective coaching that was cited by some of our most improved leaders involved the coach *providing frank feedback*.

Of course, these leaders all received lots of feedback from their coworkers at the outset of the leadership development experience—in the form of a formal 360-degree feedback report. So what sort of value-added feedback could one's coach provide? There are at least three, in our opinion. First, a well-prepared coach will know a leader's feedback so well that the coach can remind the leader of salient feedback at specific points in a coaching conversation. Second, as a leader and his or her coach are discussing what a leader has done since the previous coaching conversation (the "successes and challenges" part of a coaching meeting described above), the coach can certainly provide feedback on why he or she thinks some approaches are working while others aren't. And we saw data in our interviews related to each of these types of feedback from one's coach.

The third type of feedback that we as coaches seek to provide, and which we saw evidence of in our interviews, is a bit more tricky. We call this "real-time feedback," and it involves looking for examples of behavior from the leader that may help illustrate some aspect of his or her feedback—and looking for them *during the coaching conversations*. Then, of course, the harder part is mustering the courage, and having the tact, to constructively provide that feedback to the leader at that very moment.

This does not happen in every coaching relationship, but when it does, it can be very powerful, and there were indeed some instances of this happening with our most improved leaders. One such example came from a leader who was working on his communication style—both verbal and nonverbal. During this leader's interview, he said, "My coach made a comment about how 'Just the way you are sitting right now says something about the way people perceive you.'" In this example, the leader was sitting with a very closed body posture, a behavior that was at least consistent with some feedback he had gotten that he needed to improve in the area of openness and approachability. Being caught in the act, so to speak, was perhaps a bit awkward—but sometimes that's what it takes to get a leader to really understand how he or she is coming across to others.

In another example, a leader had received plenty of feedback from her colleagues about being too passive and conflict-avoidant when it came to tough issues—and as it turned out her coach was able to point out—in real time during a coaching meeting—that this leader was agreeing with everything the coach was saying! When the coach mentioned this observation, the leader was forced to acknowledge that she was in fact "avoiding confrontation again like I often do" by agreeing with comments on which she actually had a slightly different point of view. The conversation then pivoted right away, much sooner that it might have otherwise, to discussing some practical strategies for how to overcome this habit.

A final way in which one's coach was seen by our leaders as being helpful was by serving as a source of encouragement and even confidence. Now it must be kept in mind that, again, all leaders in our study were high-potential, high-performing leaders. Some headed up large organizations, some were in line for very senior roles, and some were already at the peak of their careers. In other words, these were the cream of the crop, so to speak. And yet, they are only human. An amazing insight for us based on this research is the finding that a number of these leaders found this sort of support from the coach to be one of the most helpful parts of the entire leadership development experience.

Examples of this finding have been sprinkled throughout this book, but one quote from one of our most improved leaders captures this insight perfectly: "My coach helped me with my confidence, almost to the point where it seemed like he let me know it's OK to be how I am, and just to keep trying to improve." We are all wired differently; that's the beauty of diversity. And by ensuring that a significant part of the coaching dialogue is a genuine exploration of a leader's true gifts and passions, and where those intersect with the organization's needs, a coach can ensure that the leader he or she is working with comes out of the development experience not only with better skills, but also with greater self-confidence.

Practical Leadership Models

One of the authors once had an experience that illustrates the limitations of the Socratic approach to coaching that a number of our most improved leaders said they found so effective (whereby the leader primarily asks good questions to help the leader come up with his or her own solutions). The author was involved in a leadership development program with a number of other consultants from other firms. By the end of the first day, the author perceived that things were not going especially well, but he had a hard time putting his finger on what the problem was. That evening, he had dinner with one of the other consultants—a highly skilled facilitator and coach, it should be noted.

Wanting to know how to make day 2 better than day 1, the author asked the other consultant, "What thoughts do you have on improvements we can make tomorrow?" The other consultant quickly replied, asking, "What do *you* think?" To be candid, the author's gut reaction was, "Don't pull that coaching stuff on me!"

The point is that the author asking for input had already put thought into what was going on, and he felt like he didn't have a handle on it. So he was asking for the perspective of someone else—in this case, a respected colleague. This incident illustrates the limits of just being the good "question-asker" as a coach or facilitator. Sometimes, the person on the other end of such questions is actually looking for a point of view.

Fortunately, when it comes to leadership development, there is no shortage of points of view. These often come in the form of leadership models, which can be thought of as practical approaches to common leadership challenges, often backed by research, and generally framed in a way that is succinct and accompanied by some sort of graphic. We include a number of these sorts of leadership models in our leadership development programs, generally seeking to tailor the specific models we include to the client we are working with and the specific objectives of a given engagement. For the leadership development programs that our most improved leaders participated in, there were three models that were found to be particularly helpful.

Among specific leadership models that our participants claimed were especially useful, the most widely cited one was the Situational Leadership model developed by Paul Hersey, Ken Blanchard, and Dewey Johnson.[1] One of our clients has a licensing agreement with the firm that owns the intellectual property associated with the Hersey version of the model, and that model is used, with permission, in one of the high-potential leadership programs from which our sample of leaders was drawn.

One of our leaders claimed that, "The Situational Leadership model was very helpful," explaining that, "I tend to use a particular style or approach, and that doesn't work all the time." This leader noted that the training she received based on this model resulted in her being "more cognizant of the idea of needing to adjust my approach from one audience to the next." This statement, of course, gets at the essence of this very useful leadership model—the idea that effective leadership involves adapting one's style appropriately from one situation to the next.

Another leader also referred to the Situational Leadership, and stressed two things. First, she noted that the model and associated self-assessment validated that her preferred style of leadership was a "participating" style, which she realized was both a good thing, when used in the right type of situation, and a limitation, when used in the wrong type of situation. Second, she noted that at the time she was participating in the program, she was just starting to build a relationship with a new boss, and she said that the one-on-one coaching conversations helped her to figure out how to better adapt her style to her new manager. This example illustrates the synergistic effect between training and coaching that often leads to true breakthroughs in terms of leadership effectiveness.

A second model from the training that some of our most improved leaders cited as particularly helpful was a simple model related to delivering feedback—the SBI model. In this model, S refers to "Situation," B refers to "Behavior," and I refers to "Impact." So, the way this might sound when one is delivering feedback is, "In situation X, I observed you doing Y, and the impact I'm concerned it may have had is Z." At this point, it is probably wise for the feedback provider to ask the feedback recipient what his or her take is on the feedback just provided. In short, this is a succinct and nonjudgmental way of sharing feedback with someone else, in order that both parties can then have a constructive conversation about the feedback.

The thing is, it works. It can actually positively impact leaders' interactions with their coworkers, as one leader testified: "Our facilitator coach shared the SBI model with us, and I remember using that pointedly with my direct reports." In fact, this leader shared that not only did she start using the model when delivering feedback to her people, she also "walked through the model" with them, gave them some examples, and encouraged her direct reports to use it with their direct reports. So it appears that this particular part of the training not only helped the leader going through the leadership development experience to improve, but it also may have had a positive ripple effective throughout her entire organization.

A final, related model is a model developed by our firm, Avion Consulting, in order to help people have challenging conversations on the job—conversations in which there is conflict or disagreement. This model is based on what we believe is some of the best research out there in the area of conflict management. It also represents our many years of experience working with leaders and teams in organizations. And it, along with the Situational Leadership and SBI models, was cited by a number of our most improved leaders as a very useful framework. As one leader put it, "the approach our facilitator taught us regarding how to have challenging conversations helped me a lot; it was very practical."

Helpful Training Modules

Beyond specific *models* that our most improved leaders found especially impactful, there were also specific *modules* from the leadership development programs they participated in that were widely cited as very helpful. The difference between a "model" and a "module" is that the former is a framework that teaches some specific skill, while the latter is a broader topic, within which there may be one or more models. For example, a module on the topic of "Communicating with Impact" may include one or more models, such as SBI, the Avion Challenging Conversations model, and so on.

In fact, some of our most improved leaders did indeed cite some sort of "Effective Communication" module as particularly helpful, with references to the "Challenging Conversations" model in particular. But consistent with the idea that a given module may include more than one model, other leaders cited different aspects of the communication-related training they received as being key to their improvement.

One such example is especially noteworthy, as it gets at a very common challenge among high-potential, high-performing leaders. The leader in this example said that what he found most impactful from the training he attended was "when we talked about executive communication, and in particular staying results-focused." The training in this area explored the idea that some leaders, when communicating to executive audiences, tend to focus too much on process (the "how") and not enough on outcomes (the "what"). This leader's key realization from the training was that "more senior leadership probably already assumes that you know your stuff, so we should be focusing on results rather than too much on process."

Another training module that a number of our leaders identified as key to their improvement was the module related to 360-degree feedback. Our approach is to identify key ideas and suggested practices that apply to all leaders we are working with in a given group and address those in a training session, thus saving the one-on-one coaching sessions for discussions that are specific to each leader. The evidence seems to suggest that this approach generally worked well for our most improved leaders.

Two things in particular from that module really seemed to resonate with our leaders. First, they indicated that the way in which the 360-degree feedback process was set up was helpful. One leader noted that, "People can get defensive when receiving such feedback, and the way the process was set up prepared us well." More specifically, this leader emphasized a discussion during this module about how "feedback is all about perception, but perception is really important." This observation by this leader is, of course, consistent with what we argue in Chapter 1 of this book—that leadership, at its core, is very much about people's perceptions of the leader.

A second aspect of the module dealing with 360-degree feedback was the discussion of the nature and importance of "spikes," meaning areas in which a leader is not just strong, but rather *distinctive*. We deal with this topic at length in Chapter 11. For now, suffice it to say that one of our most improved leaders said that the idea he found particularly helpful from the training was "the concept of spikes," and in particular, the idea that "if you have a certain number of spikes, people will focus more on those than they will on weaknesses, provided they are mild weaknesses." This leader added that "the way this was then connected to our 360" was especially impactful.

The module that was most widely cited among our most improved leaders as having a significant impact, however, was a module on the topic of "Leading Change." In virtually every case in which one of our leaders mentioned this as the part of the training that most helped them to improve, the rationale was the same; the organization was going through a significant change, and the Leading Change module provided them with what might be thought of as just-in-time training to help them with an immediate leadership challenge.

For example, one leader stated that, "The training corresponded directly to things going on in the organization (for example, leaders getting training in Change Leadership just as the organization was going through a huge change to a new Operating Model)." Another noted that, "I think the Leading Change module was very helpful, given where we are as an organization." Finally, one leader said, "The Leading Change topic was good for me because I knew that I would be going into the Operating Model project and what a big change that would be." This leader further explained that the part of that training that was especially helpful was the segment on "Building the case for change" and "telling the story—who, what, why, how." This leader concluded with the statement, "It was all about the timing."

In short, well-crafted leadership training modules that include practical models related to real and current challenges that leaders are facing apparently can contribute significantly to the improvement of leaders. And when combined with 360-degree feedback and one-on-one coaching, we believe—and the evidence seems to support—that there is a synergistic effect among these leadership development strategies. The whole, in other words, is greater than the sum of its parts. But there is another facet of these programs that, for some of our leaders, really brought everything together: The Leadership Project.

Business Project

In the field of leadership development, there is a term for an approach to training that combines content (models, best practices, and so on) with an opportunity to immediately apply the content one is learning. That term is *action learning,* and we are increasingly coming to believe that it is an approach that should be incorporated into efforts to help leaders improve whenever possible. For some of our leaders, the form that this approach took was a "leadership project" that they worked on over the course of the leadership development program they were participating in.

Here was the idea. At the outset of the six-month leadership development program, each leader came up with an idea for a business project. Early in the program, a model was shared for translating the idea into an actual business case, which was used for getting approval from key decision-makers for proceeding with the project, and/or for getting buy-in from key stakeholders when it came to actually executing. The project then became part of the focus of subsequent training sessions and one-on-one coaching sessions. To illustrate, instead of talking about adapting one's leadership style in the abstract, we would talk about how to tailor one's style to specific coworkers with whom the leader needed to be able to work effectively in order to successfully execute one's project.

Based on what we learned from our most improved leaders, this really worked. One leader noted that, "The development experience was tied to an actual work application (the business project)," and another pointed out that, "We were held accountable for doing that work" (since they had to present the results of their projects at the end of the program) and that the project "gave us a chance to practice the methods we were learning in the workshops and coaching sessions." Finally, one leader argued that, "I've been in other leadership development programs both here and elsewhere, and the difference with this one was that the process was woven into the work we are doing, since we were doing a project directly related to our work."

We believe this feedback from leaders regarding the importance of working on projects over the course of a leadership development experience, and being able to actually apply what they are learning from their feedback, training, and coaching in the context of these projects, gets right at the heart of what this study is all about. In other words, most people reading this book have probably participated in leadership development experiences that were informative, thought-provoking, and maybe even entertaining.

But we don't believe that an organization is getting its return on investment if leaders come out of such experiences having merely been informed or entertained. The goal, in our view, is actual improvement. And we have concluded that helping leaders immediately apply what they are learning to a real and current leadership challenge, such as successfully leading some sort of organizational change, is a great way of ensuring that the leaders we are working with are actually improving. In fact, one way of ensuring that leaders participating in such a program take the project aspect of the program very seriously is to ensure that it has lots of visibility with senior leadership—which, interestingly, is yet another thing that our most improved leaders cited as a factor that helped explain their improvement.

Visibility with Senior Leadership

In our experience, it is sadly often the case that senior leadership sees "leadership training and development" as something that is for all leaders—starting at the level right below themselves. In fact, as of the writing of this chapter, all three of the authors are involved in a large engagement with a client for which the senior leadership team is, on one hand, agreeing to significantly fund a broad leadership development initiative, but on the other hand, declining to personally participate in a significant portion of that leadership development.

Of course, personally participating in leadership development efforts is just one way in which senior leaders can ensure that they are meaningfully contributing to leadership effectiveness within their organizations. Another way is to support the leadership development efforts of their would-be successors in various ways. When it comes to the programs that our most improved leaders were participating in, there were two forms of support from senior leaders that our leaders said were helpful to their improvement—both dealing with exposure to senior executives.

The first pertains to the business projects discussed above. At the end of the six-month leadership development experience, participants present the results of their projects in front of all of their managers, as well as Executive Leadership Team.

And the participants love it (though some would probably say they have a love–hate relationship with it, since it understandably can be a bit stressful for some). As one leader put it, "My presentation at the end of [the program] was so timely, since I wouldn't normally get a lot of exposure to senior management." This person added that, because of the nature of his project, the presentation gave him and his team a "chance to sell our internal capability."

Another leader echoed the sentiment, stating that, "The added exposure from the program helped." This person then elaborated by noting that, "The COO saw my name on the presentations program, as did my boss (who reported to the COO), and they knew I was taking this seriously." He then added that, "The way [the Chief Executive Officer] reacted to my presentation was great; he said, 'I like these slides—we should use these slides.'"

We think these comments illustrate two different ways in which this exposure to senior management at the end of the leadership development experience helped drive improvement on the part of our leaders. First, knowing throughout the entire program that they would have to present to senior management on the results of a project caused them to take the projects very seriously, which meant taking the entire program seriously. Second, actually doing the presentations and getting positive feedback from the executives served as a form of recognition; it motivated our leaders, built their confidence, and just generally fostered their engagement.

Beyond attending the project presentations session at the end of the program, there was another way in which senior leaders supported our participants' development efforts: typically each program workshop was kicked off by a different senior leader. And the senior leaders almost invariably took this responsibility very seriously. For example, they were informed well in advance about what the topic was for the session they would be kicking off, and they almost always came in with great advice in that area, poignant stories to illustrate their advice, and so on. One of our leaders conveyed the sentiments of numerous others, saying, "Being able to interact with the CFO and other senior leaders at the start of each session was extremely valuable."

Structured Follow-up Process

One final aspect of the training experience that our most improved leaders widely cited as helping them improve was the structured follow-up process that was clearly outlined for them early in the program. While it has long been known that there is a strong relationship between follow-up and improvement, we have noticed two extremes over the years.

On one hand, we have at times been exposed to leadership development efforts in which the importance of follow-up is clearly communicated, but not very much is done to actually help participants put in place a game plan for following up. On the other hand, we have seen some efforts to help people follow up that are so cumbersome that participants see them as more of a hassle than an enabler. We, of course, have tried to strike the right balance between trying to provide sufficient structure without seeming to over-engineer the process.

Our most improved leaders seem to think that the structured follow-up process was truly an enabler—something that helped account for their improvement. As one leader responded when asked to account for his significant improvement, "I analyzed my 360, made a plan, communicated it, and got feedback throughout the process." Another leader had a similar response, saying, "The 360 alone isn't enough; the keys are awareness, planning, and then execution." Finally, one leader referred to the helpfulness of the "Action-planning, follow-up, tools, and templates to help us be effective at following up" and added that these features were "Not as mature in other leadership programs" he had participated in.

Conclusion

Two key thoughts come to mind as we wrap up this chapter on training experience. First, to be very candid, we have felt a bit uneasy while writing this chapter, since it may come across more as an effort to promote our firm and our approach to leadership training than we intend it to be. All we can say is that many of our most improved leaders did indeed indicate that there were aspects of the training part of their experience that they truly thought helped account for their improvement. So, as much as possible, we are simply trying to reflect what they said they actually found helpful.

Second, someone reading this chapter might wonder: Didn't the leaders who weren't among your most improved leaders go through the same training experiences? And, if so, can you really say that those training experiences helped account for why your most improved leaders got better?

We think these are very fair questions, and we agree that, perhaps more so than any of the previous insights in this book (dealing with ripeness, the central issue, the guiding metaphor, and so on), the training experience was similar across all participants—both the most improved leaders and the leaders who didn't improve so much. However, in our minds the key is not that our most improved leaders went through the training experience; the key is how they reacted to it.

Did they really seek and get full value out of the coaching sessions, or did they go through the motions? Did they actually apply the leadership models they learned in the workshops, or was it "business as usual" as soon as they got back to their offices? Did they actually use the structured follow-up process that was provided to them, or did they constantly fail to take the steps that they were encouraged to take?

Let us close with an example. In a recent group of leaders that we worked with, there was one particular leader who, frankly, did a horrible job of using the follow-up process that we advocated. He was a nice guy, very smart, and very accomplished. But he did not go through a single one of the follow-up steps that we taught. He never did get around to developing an action plan; he didn't have follow-up conversations with the people who provided feedback; he didn't go through the steps we identified for socializing his project idea. He wasn't a jerk about it; it just never seemed to be a priority for him. And how would you guess his follow-up feedback looked?

We predicted that he would not make it into our "most improved leader" sample, and we were right. In fact, that's an understatement; he had the worst follow-up feedback of anyone in that group (and some of the worst follow-up feedback we can recall). And, again, it was utterly predictable. So while all leaders had access to the same sorts of leadership training experiences, not all leaders took equal advantage of the opportunities to grow and develop that they had right in front of them.

Recommendations

For the Leader

- Anticipate that you will find several aspects of training valuable, including specific content, some part of the process (for example, learning from peers with similar challenges), and of course the specific things that apply to you individually (for example, your 360-degree feedback).

- Be sure to create an action plan based on your feedback and learning, and—just as importantly—have a plan for following up on your efforts after the program/process is over.

- If you are not getting as much value out of an overall leadership development process or program as you would like, focus on the aspects of the process that hold the most value for you (for example, interacting with peers with similar challenges, getting exposure to senior leaders, etc.).

- Recognize that a good leadership development process has several parts that combine to impact your development; pay attention to how these different aspects of the program/process—training, coaching, assessment, feedback, etc.—combine or intersect (rather than thinking of them as separate).

- If your action areas are skill-related, find specific training that deals with those skills.
- Consider what training you've already been through (no doubt you will have to go back and refresh your memory), and apply those concepts to your action areas.

For the Organization

- Involve senior leaders who are not actual participants in a leadership development program and find a way to involve them, since doing so signals the value of the program and inspires participants to take the learning seriously.
- Help senior leaders prepare for their involvement—whether that involvement includes speaking at sessions, serving as an audience for project presentations, or some other activity—so that they are well prepared to deliver the message and impact the program participants need.
- Avoid leadership development efforts that operate in isolation or that just focus on classroom time; invest in processes and programs that include training, coaching, assessment, feedback, and action learning—and in which there is a real-world connection to the business strategy.
- Consider both internal training solutions and external opportunities.
- If similar strength and developmental themes emerge across leaders, find training that meets organizational-level needs.

For the Coach

- Set expectations for leaders who are being trained that there are clear "best practices" for how to be a good "consumer" of training (based on the research here and elsewhere).
- Stress the importance of the combined value of the various components of the leader's development experience; talk to the leader about previous successes (and failures) of past leaders; show the payoffs and pitfalls of engaging in all aspects of the process/program.
- Recommend only training programs—within and outside the organization—that are high quality and provide most (or at least some) of the factors known to deliver value to leaders and their organizations.

CHAPTER NINE

Social Support

In Chapters 2 and 3, we argued that the "ripeness" of a leader is a key determinant of improvement, and we defined *ripeness* as a leader's readiness to improve, either in general or in a particular area. We then distinguished between intrinsic (inside out) and extrinsic (outside in) ripeness factors, and we noted that the outside-in ripeness factors that surfaced in our research included potential for advancement, professional transitions, organizational changes, and other timing-related variables.

Of course, if a leader is actually going to improve, at some point he or she must move from being ripe ("I'm ready to go!") to actually *improving*. And we found that external factors (people, opportunities, environmental conditions, and so on) not only served as a catalyst that impacted the ripeness of our most improved leaders, but also enhanced the effectiveness of their efforts to then actually improve.

Several types of external factors were cited by our most improved leaders, but social support from others in the organization was by far the most widely cited external factor that fostered improvement. Social support came from a variety of sources, including mentors, coaches, peers, supervisors, and even non-work sources. Collectively, these individuals helped our most improved leaders to take meaningful steps in their development journeys.

Why Is Social Support Beneficial?

One of the common challenges of being a consultant is the weight gain caused by too many rich dinners coupled with too little exercise. Racing to catch a flight, scant or substandard hotel gym equipment, unpredictable schedules and late nights of work are known to take their toll on consultants' waistlines. Such was the case for one of the authors, who one day stepped on the scale and found himself 20 pounds heavier than at any other point in his life. He had heard about Weight Watchers from a relative and decided to give it a try. Since this decision, the author has lost 40 pounds and adopted a new, healthier way to eat, enabling him to sustain his weight loss.

In the author's opinion, there were two keys to the effectiveness of Weight Watchers in his weight loss efforts. The first was informational in nature. Weight Watchers taught the author the mechanics of an improved diet. At the time the author attended Weight Watchers, he learned that every portion or meal had a point value associated with it, and each person, depending on his or her weight and activity level, was afforded a certain daily point total. By not exceeding this point total, people lose weight in a healthy and sustainable way.

However, at least in general terms, the author already knew what constituted a healthy diet. In the author's opinion, the magic of the Weight Watchers program was the social support that was a significant part of the program. On a weekly basis, members would come together for weekly "weigh ins" to review progress, discuss setbacks, and identify strategies for incorporating a healthy diet into one's lifestyle. The social support of the group was the key ingredient in the program—it helped to bring these dietary changes to life for the members attending the program.

Further, Weight Watchers offered free lifetime memberships to members who had sustained a healthy lifestyle for a certain period of time. These individuals served as role models or mentors to the other members of the group. Collectively, this social support from a cohort group experiencing the same challenges enabled the dietary changes to come to life and become healthier habits for the author.

Employee wellness initiatives are designed such that they also leverage the positive impact that social support can have in workplace health promotion initiatives. For example, one of the authors coached a senior leader in a *Fortune* 500 insurance provider. This particular organization had a wellness program in which individuals were provided with Fitbits in order to track their weekly steps. Those who exceeded a certain number of steps on a weekly basis received a healthcare stipend that reduced the amount that the employees needed to pay for their insurance. Leaders and departments were encouraged to participate in "activity competitions" with other departments: The department that took the most collective steps in a given time period won a valued outcome such as an afternoon off or a company-sponsored social event.

The number of times that the author heard employees at this organization discussing their steps in a given day was remarkable. For example, when teammates were waiting for the elevator, teammates walking through the hall encouraged them to take the stairs as an easy way to get some steps in. When considering where to go for lunch, the number of steps was often considered. Employees frequently discussed their step totals with one another.

The author wondered what was happening here, as he had had a Fitbit for years and never had this level of commitment to counting his steps. Undoubtedly, the social support from the organization was playing an important role in helping these people change their behaviors. In fact, the research around health promotion in the workplace strongly emphasizes the role that social support plays in enabling people to change long-standing habits regarding their physical activity.[1] Similarly, our most improved leaders often mentioned social support as an important element in their improvement.

All of this raises the question: How does social support assist us in making such behavior changes? Researchers have long observed a link between social support and behavior change, and literature in this area often focuses on the distinction between "perceived" and "received" support.[2]

Perceived support can be thought of as the belief that one has assistance available to him or her if needed. To illustrate, one leader we worked with was focused on being a more empowering manager. This leader, however, was concerned that enhanced empowerment of direct reports would lead to her having a reduced ability to accurately answer the pointed, detailed questions her manager directed her way on a regular basis. The leader we were working with discussed this reservation with her manager, who indicated that she was supportive of the efforts the leader was making to empower her direct reports more.

Further, provided the leader got back to her in timely manner, the manager indicated that she would be open to the leader saying "I need to connect with 'so and so' and get back to you with an answer ASAP." This support represents perceived support, because the manager had alleviated the leader's concerns on an as-needed basis. In this case, the perceived support likely impacted the leader's confidence or security in making the change by negotiating or strategizing the perceived negative outcomes of making the change in advance of actually making the behavior change.

Received support, on the other hand, refers to the actual provision of support (that is, providing an article, giving feedback, listening, etc.). For example, one of our most improved leaders, who had been a manager in operations, indicated that all of her supervisors believed and expressed she was ready for "the next step." This leader's supervisor was clearly providing motivation, or encouraging goal attainment, by trusting and uplifting the leader we were working with. This leader also received development support from her manager through direct guidance during the leadership development program. This leader stated, "My boss and his boss are very good leaders. They lead by example. Just listening to him have conversations was helpful because he is so skilled. And he has encouraged my development." The supervisor's encouragement, role modeling, and provision of recommendations and advice represents received support.

Behavior change science indicates that both perceived and received support are at least somewhat correlated with behavior change.[3] Interestingly, however, perceived support appears to be more predictive of behavior change than is received support. In other words, the belief that one has about others' anticipated support on an as-needed basis appears to be even more predictive of behavior change than is actual, received support.

Collectively, both perceived and received social support enable behavior change through four different channels,[4] all of which were reflected by our most improved leaders.

- Emotional Support (Empathy, nurturance, inspiration, and encouragement)
- Tangible Support (concrete methods of support, including money, resources, and services, such as an executive coach or an additional direct report)
- Informational Support (advice, guidance, or suggestions)
- Companionship Support (sense of belonging, a sense of "we-ness")

Emotional Support

One form of social support is emotional support, or behavior that is intended to encourage or build the confidence of another person. Such behaviors can include listening, providing positive feedback, encouraging someone, or validating another's thoughts or ideas. For example, one of our most improved leaders desired reassurance and positive feedback that the changes she was making were working. The leader shared: "It's been extremely helpful to have my manager as a mentor when challenges come up. He reassures me [through] positive feedback." This encouragement resulted in the manager helping our leader to overcome confidence barriers, which are often encountered in the midst of change, and resulted in the leader we were working with believing that she had the inherent attributes necessary for success.

Early on in one of the author's careers, a colleague provided meaningful emotional social support that went a surprisingly long way toward maximizing his performance. The author and his colleague (with whom he had worked extensively) were going to facilitate a leadership development program with very senior members of an investment bank. For readers who have not had exposure to leaders in this industry, suffice it to say that this is a sophisticated and demanding audience. Below are the author's recollections of the interaction.

The night before the session, my colleague saw me reviewing flashcards with some of the key points I hoped to emphasize in the following day's session. The colleague asked me why I was reviewing the flashcards. I explained that I wanted to be on my "A-game" tomorrow. The colleague chuckled and said that I knew the particular content we would be covering the next day backward and forward and that I didn't need to review the flashcards. This encouragement struck just the right chord with me as, deep down, I knew he was right. The session the following day was a success, in part due to the additional confidence my colleague had triggered in me.

On one hand, the "you got this" message that the colleague had provided to the author was not a particularly sophisticated or complicated idea. On the other hand, the comment struck just the right chord with the author. The colleague had taken the time to surface and listen to the author's concerns. He knew the author's capabilities, both generally as a facilitator and specifically in the particular content areas. Furthermore, the colleague was subtly encouraging the author not to worry. Collectively, these attributes of emotional social support enabled the author to "have his A-game" the next day.

Tangible Support

A second form of social support is what is referred to as tangible support. This includes the concrete supporting behaviors that others can engage in to help improve performance. For example, providing access to an administrative assistant for a leader who is overextended is a form of tangible support, as is providing an executive coach or hiring an extra direct report to enhance a leader's bandwidth.

Our most improved leaders discussed some examples in which the provision of tangible support enabled them to lead more effectively. For example, one leader cited an example in which her boss provided a tangible form of social support. This individual was a leader in healthcare, with responsibility for supporting over 120 clinical practices throughout her region. Her 360-degree feedback report highlighted the need for her to build stronger relationships with a broader set of the practices she was responsible for supporting. She was disappointed to learn that a number of her feedback providers indicated that they did not find her to be responsive to the needs of their practices.

In part, this was driven by cost-containment efforts that restricted her ability to travel to all the offices in her region. When this leader reviewed her feedback with her manager, he indicated that he would be willing to financially support more travel to the various offices in her region, as well as invest in webinar technology and training in order to enable remote learning. Both of these investments represented tangible support, and they enabled the leader to respond meaningfully to her feedback. As a result, she proved to be one of our most improved leaders.

Informational Support

A third form of social support is what is referred to as informational support. *Informational support* refers to the provision of advice, guidance, or suggestions that enable a leader to enhance his or her skills. Our most improved leaders frequently cited this form of social support as a critical aspect of their development, often indicating that a coach or internal mentor had provided them with guidance or direction that was quite helpful.

For example, one of our most improved leaders identified an individual to be his mentor because he wanted to learn a specific content area from that particular individual. In particular, the individual was focused on building his presentation skills, and the mentor he identified modeled exceptional communication skills (for example, storytelling during presentations). As a result of this mentoring experience, the leader learned a variety of best practices regarding presentations that he successfully put into practice in his subsequent presentations.

This example illustrates once again the impact that a role model demonstrating a desired behavior can have, not just for the recipient, but also for those who will be impacted by the recipient's future behavior. Another leader in our study further illustrated with the following example: "I just had surgery on my neck a week ago. I got a text from my senior leader saying, 'I just want to let you know I'm thinking about you. Sleep in and get some rest tomorrow.'" Not only was this a considerate gesture, but it also role-modeled the behaviors a thoughtful leader would engage in.

Another source of informational support cited by our most improved leaders was one's external leadership coach. For some, the objectivity of the coach as a provider of guidance and information was perceived to make a difference. A coach's objectivity can be particularly helpful when we understand that leaders often experience pressures or receive messages from their organizations to lead in specific, culturally consistent ways. Yet leaders may believe that these development goals are inconsistent with their values or way of being. Coaching can provide the opportunity to craft more personally relevant forms of leadership that still correspond to the organization's needs and competencies.

One of our most improved leaders, for instance, reflected on the objectivity of coaching, stating: "The one-on-one coaching sessions were meaningful. It was helpful to get my coach's insights, because my coach was not engrained in our culture. This allowed him to offer fresh perspectives, to challenge me to think of things differently, and to offer good advice."

Although our most improved leaders cited numerous examples of informational social support proving useful in enhancing their skills, for several reasons it is our belief and experience that many leaders and coaches tend to overly rely on this form of social support. First, as we reviewed in our chapter on Ripeness, providing advice, guidance, and direction is not likely to be useful or impactful until one is "ripe" to make the change. If you've ever found yourself thinking, "if only so-and-so would just listen to my advice he or she would be fine," only to find that so-and-so rejects your advice for what you find to be noncompelling reasons, you know exactly what we mean.

However, when a leader is ripe for change, he or she is *looking* for answers and *striving* to lead more effectively. Thus, those who are ripe may wish to have heard the profound advice earlier in their career, without sufficiently appreciating the role that their ripeness played to begin with. This emphasis on answers rather than ripeness causes many well-intentioned leaders and coaches to focus on providing forms of informational social support (such as giving advice) rather than ripening the leader. These well-intentioned coaches and managers would be well served to heed the old saying, "when the student is ready, the teacher will appear."

A second caveat about informational social support should be emphasized, which is that the individual offering the informational support (for example, advice, guidance, and direction) must be careful to promote a sense of personal accountability or ownership in the leader rather than dependency. We have witnessed many well-intentioned managers or coaches who are quick to jump in and provide answers or directions to an individual who is looking to make a behavior change (for example, "you should delegate project X to so-and-so"). Advice of this nature may expediently address the problem at hand. However, it is not the most expedient method of development, as it fails to promote an individual's independent thinking and often leaves the leader dependent on his or her manager's or coach's guidance.

Indeed, such advice-giving may result in the leader's lack of personal commitment or accountability to the change being suggested. In summary, although our most improved leaders frequently mentioned informational social support as a factor that helps explain their improvement, we believe this is best viewed as a form of support that dovetails well with other forms of support, rather than as simply a great stand-alone recommendation.

Companionship Support

The final form of social support that our most improved leaders cited as beneficial is what is referred to as "companionship social support." This form of social support refers to a sense of belonging to a group with shared experiences or challenges. Of late, we have witnessed a proliferation of affinity coaching groups in the organizations and industries we serve. For example, many female leaders in investment banking have joined the WOWS Group (Women of Wall Street), a collection of female leaders who regularly come together for networking and development purposes. Despite the considerable personal and professional time demands of many of these female leaders, they invest some of their precious discretionary time to attend these meetings. One of the reasons affinity groups such as WOWS are proliferating is the opportunity it offers to discuss shared challenges with peers who bring diverse ideas and perspectives to common challenges.

Similarly, our most improved leaders frequently cited companionship social support as an important aspect of their development (although they referred to it as peer-to-peer relationships rather than companionship social support). We can acknowledge the sense of relatedness, both positive and negative, experienced by peers in a leadership development program. It takes high levels of self-awareness, honesty, and courage to confront development opportunities. So, having people who can directly relate to such an experience undoubtedly provides support, motivation, and the foundation to meet those development goals.

For some leaders, it was incredibly helpful for them to have someone to vent to, or release their frustrations with. As one of our most improved leaders indicated, "Kids get locked up in a school for eight hours then they want to explode. Changing your behavior at work is the same way— sometimes you need to vent. Having a peer that knows that and is not always coaching you is important. I have a peer who is like that for me. We balance each other." This is an exceptional articulation of the value of companionship social support.

Another example represents an intersection of companionship and informational social support. The leader in this example was a new mother who had identified as a mentor a working mom whom she felt balanced home and work in an admirable and effective manner. This leader described her mentor recommending relevant leadership books and sharing useful advice. The leader noted that she appreciated the ability her mentor had to relate to her experience as a mother and leader. Thus, while books and advice (informational social support) may have been useful, the fact that the mentor was a role model working mom (companionship social support) was important to the ideas being perceived as credible to begin with.

Support from Coaches

As noted previously, the support provided by our most improved leaders' coaches was frequently cited as a key variable explaining how our leaders improved. As discussed in the preceding chapter on one's "Training Experience," coaching helped many of our most improved leaders set goals, determine personal action steps, and receive general support and challenge from a consistent and perhaps more objective person. We would like to emphasize a couple elements of this coaching that strike us a relevant to this chapter on social support.

Many leaders attributed the consistent nature of the coaching relationship as being a catalyst that set in motion their development. Some leaders compared the leadership development programs in which they were involved, including the coaching sessions, to other training or feedback programs they had previously participated in. They reported that the ongoing nature of the coaching and training support over a six-month to one-year period (as opposed to the common "one-and-done" approach to training) significantly contributed to their ability to improve as leaders. Trust and understanding take time to develop. As a result, ongoing coaching and training relationships, and consistent development cohort groups, are more compelling forms of support than are one-time leadership development events.

An additional advantage that a coach has over an internal stakeholder is that the feedback the coach delivers may also be viewed as more objective and, thus, more sincere. Among our most improved leaders, this perception of objectivity often facilitated leaders taking the feedback more to heart because they viewed the feedback as coming from someone who did not have ulterior motives. One leader said of his coach, "It was great to have that third party, objective person to take a broader view of my style, and to provide frank feedback."

The final point regarding coaches and social support we'd like to emphasize is that over the authors' collective 50-plus years of coaching experience, we have come to greatly appreciate the importance of involving internal stakeholders throughout the coaching engagement. Our engagements with specific leaders are time-limited, usually lasting between 6 and 12 months. We certainly believe that meaningful progress can be made throughout the course of a coaching engagement. However, for three reasons, we routinely involve the sponsor throughout the coaching engagement.

First, the perspective of the sponsor (usually the participating leader's boss) regarding the goals and the priorities of the engagement are of paramount importance. When coaching occurs in a vacuum and doesn't incorporate the sponsors' perspectives regarding goals and priorities, the wrong central issue may be addressed. For example, one leader we've worked with received two core feedback messages: she was long-winded and her decision-making was not sufficiently based on data. Being perceived as long-winded really stung for this leader, and being more succinct was the primary area of focus in her coaching.

However, unbeknownst to her and her coach at the time, her decision-making being insufficiently based on data was the far greater issue for her manager. At the conclusion of the engagement, the boss did not perceive that the leader had made much progress on the issue that mattered to him. Involving the boss consistently throughout the coaching engagement would have helped to avoid this unfortunate outcome. This may seem self-evident. However, a great many leaders we've worked with fail to demonstrate this proactivity and candor with their bosses.

Second, involving the sponsor often results in the provision of "calibrating feedback" for the coach and the participating leader. Leaders may under- or overestimate the impact of their behavior change efforts, and feedback from a sponsor can help to calibrate one's efforts. Those who have worked as executive coaches know that they are very dependent on the participating leader's perceptions of his or her own progress and change. Thus, involvement of the participating leader's boss provides new perspective and valuable insights regarding the effectiveness of the behavior changes being made.

Finally, and most importantly, coaching is designed to be a time-limited intervention. We typically have between 6 and 12 months to assist a leader with the changes he or she is seeking to make. By involving the sponsor throughout the course of the engagement, the coach is building a strategy to transition support from coach to manager. Candor and openness regarding the leader's development is established, which makes the handoff far smoother, and this is critical to minimizing the possibility of "relapsing" back to the status quo at the conclusion of the engagement. Of course, the confidentiality of the coaching discussions needs to be honored. However, we have found it very feasible to balance the confidentiality of coaching discussions with managerial involvement in the coaching goals and objectives.

Support from Non-Work Sources

Development does not occur in a vacuum. In our experience, development goals that show up at work are frequently consistent with challenges that a leader may be having at home, as well. For example, the leader who doesn't listen effectively at work is also quite likely to be seen as a less-than-stellar listener at home. While we recognize and agree that one of the broad-brush strokes that differentiates coaching from therapy is a focus on workplace performance, we also have found it helpful to have leaders explore how close connections in their personal lives can augment their development efforts at work. In other words, despite the need to establish clear coaching boundaries, we believe the provision of social support is not and should not be limited to those at work.

Quite a few of our most improved leaders shared that individuals in their personal lives also provided social support that facilitated their improvement. For example, a self-identified introverted leader indicated that her father, also an introvert, provided a push toward action during the leadership development program. This push served to both corroborate the area of focus (outspoken thought leadership) and motivate the leader to make targeted changes in her leadership approach. Given the closeness of the leader and her father, the alignment of their values, and the rapport they share, this social support was particularly powerful for the leader.

Involvement of non-work sources of social support deepens the development process through personalization and ownership. The social support figures are typically highly credible and understand the leader's motivations, aspirations, and strengths and developmental areas far better than their work colleagues or their coaches do. Of course, the coach cannot mandate that the leader seek social support from personal stakeholders, but the coach *can* explore it and perhaps encourage the leader to discuss his or her feedback and action plans with personal life stakeholders.

In summary, social support proved to be a key factor that helped our most improved leaders make meaningful progress on their development goals. Specifically, we found examples of four different forms of social support in our data: emotional support, tangible support, informational support, and companionship support. Further, our most improved leaders indicated that a wide range of people, including leadership coaches, cohort groups, managers, peers, direct reports, and even non-work sources provided the support they received. So, while it may not necessarily take an entire village in order for a leader to improve, it certainly seems to be the case that enlisting the support of at least a few fellow villagers can help!

Recommendations

For the Leader

- Seek strategies to involve others in your development. For example, identify a trusted individual who has already worked on issues similar to yours and ask if he or she will be willing to serve as a sounding board for you as you work on your action plan.
- Find someone who is both credible to you and capable of pushing you in ways that are not counterproductive.
- If your organization has a formal mentor program, use this as a way to get connected with someone to help you address your action plan.
- Reflect on how your feedback themes (strengths and weaknesses) show up outside of work and consider exploring your feedback themes and action plan with trusted non-work stakeholders.
- If participating in an ongoing development program, consider scheduling meetings with your cohort group to support one another's development.

For the Organization

- Consider implementing a mentoring program. Identify individuals who would be willing to serve as mentors and the particular areas of expertise in which they would feel comfortable mentoring.
- Build interaction into your training and coaching programs to promote social support.
- Leverage affinity groups such as women's leadership, millennial leaders, or minority leadership groups.
- Get HR involved in the coaching process as internal advisors.
- Create "buddy systems" in training programs by pairing individuals with the same one or two colleagues over the course of the program or initiative. Furthermore, encourage these buddy-group discussions to continue back in the workplace.
- Create group development cohort groups. Identify high-frequency development areas (such as public speaking, difficult discussions, or transitioning leaders) and invite employees with developmental goals in these areas to attend the cohort group. However, rather than simply delivering quality training content that highlights a series of best practices, encourage the group members to discuss their challenges and their own experiences and to provide support to one another.

- Structure training so that the same set of individuals goes through a set of training courses together in order to enhance the quality of social support provided (through greater trust and understanding).
- Build in managerial support and involvement throughout a coaching engagement. Specifically, we recommend involving one's manager in the review of the post-feedback action plan, a midpoint progress review, and a coaching handoff discussion at the conclusion of the engagement.

For the Coach

- Ask leaders questions that help them think about who else they should rely on to execute their leadership development plans.
- Be intentional about who matches well with whom, from both a content perspective and a style perspective.
- Indicate to your leader that you'd like to support their behavior change efforts and inquire as to what forms of support he or she would find helpful.
- Utilize the RIPEN framework to assist individuals to be ready to hear or seek out advice or recommendations. Don't provide advice or specific direction until it is requested.
- Rather than providing your strategy for success, see the world through your leader's eyes by inquiring about why the desired behavior is challenging for the individual. Work with the leader on action plans to guard against these idiosyncratic barriers.

CHAPTER TEN

Keep It Real
(with Yourself and Others)

Consider the power that comes from hearing a leader acknowledge to others that he or she has room for improvement. Hopefully, most of us can identify a leader who has demonstrated this sort of openness and authenticity at some point in our careers.

Here's one of our own examples. Not too long ago, we had the CEO of one of the organizations we serve come and "kick off" off one of our leadership development programs, and in addition to the typical opening remarks that a senior leader might deliver in this type of situation, this CEO also publicly shared one of his own development areas. He not only spoke about the specific issue, but he also acknowledged that he continues to struggle with the issue, even though he has worked at it and improved over time. He then commented that, "None of us are perfect, so each of us must strive to improve ourselves as leaders for the benefit of our people."

Not only was this demonstration of self-awareness and humility admirable, it probably inspired others to be more open about their own development areas. In addition, we believe it simultaneously communicated a sense that it was OK to be imperfect, while also creating an expectation that everyone should be striving to improve over the course of the leadership development program.

Another insight we want to share from our research suggests that what this CEO did is illustrative of a quality that was consistently exhibited by our most improved leaders: A sense of humility and authenticity about one's own development, or what we have come to refer to as "keeping it real." More specifically, we have come to believe that a key driver of improvement is a sincere belief and acknowledgement, both with oneself and with others, that we are all imperfect. As such, leaders should always be striving to cultivate a greater sense of self-awareness.

Now, as we explore how our most improved leaders put the idea of keeping it real into action, it's important to remember that self-awareness is not just about self-perceptions, since leaders' self-perceptions are often different from how others perceive them. In our experience, leaders frequently perceive the way in which they are communicating future plans, implementing decisions, and upholding values differently from how others perceive them in these areas. Thus, true self-awareness means not only that I have a sense of what makes me tick, but also that I have a sense of how others see me.

Let us put it this way. If a leader tells you he or she is fully self-aware, then goes on to disagree with consistent feedback received from numerous stakeholders, or disputes the relevance of the opinions of colleagues, then we would suggest that this leader is not truly demonstrating full

Figure 10.1

self-awareness. To be self-aware means to not only consider your views of yourself, but also to incorporate fully the views of those around you. Thus, to be truly self-aware means that you are being authentic with yourself in acknowledging that others' viewpoints regarding your leadership behavior matter. Remember what we said very early on in this book: leadership is a perceived phenomenon, so if you think you are a great leader but others don't—by definition, they are right!

In short, our most improved leaders demonstrated authenticity about their strengths *and* their development areas to both *themselves* (through Self-Awareness and a Commitment to Improve) and to *others* (through Transparency and Following up with Others). (See Figure 10.1). This mental and behavioral authenticity is what we call "keeping it real."

Authenticity with Self

Self-Awareness

We view self-awareness as the ability to be introspective, reflecting on self-perceptions and others' perceptions as well. Without the ability to be introspective or to receive feedback, it would be difficult for leaders to know what skills, behaviors, or content knowledge they should improve or address. In reviewing our data, self-awareness that came from the feedback process provided leaders with a better understanding of themselves and helped them realize how they were impacting other people.

Indeed, when we compare our research findings during the "How Leaders Improve" project to our years of experience coaching and training thousands of leaders across the globe, we see amazing consistency in the value of helping leaders become more self-aware by providing them feedback from the people they work with. Many leaders have some form of a blind spot, and by exposing those blind spots leaders can then choose to take action. But until they are made aware of their impact on others, there is no chance that a leader will magically wake up one day and think they must change their behavior.

As discussed above, self-awareness is not just about how leaders see themselves; rather, it is also about recognizing how *others* see and experience them. This is particularly important when we consider the discrepancies and/or biases that leaders—like all people—naturally hold. And even if they do not hold these discrepancies and/or biases, leaders are often evaluated on how they impact others, and organizational health and success rests in large part on leaders who consider the impact they have on others.

Our most improved leaders seemed to acknowledge the importance of developing self-awareness through the leadership development process.

One of them put it this way: "Self-awareness was at the forefront of every conversation I engaged in" after having received feedback as a part of the development process. This leader then added that, "When my 360 results came back I saw a theme—something I was already aware of—and it helped me by just keeping me more self-aware of it as I interacted with people." It may not be easy or even pleasant to keep an area for development in mind during virtually every interaction with one's coworkers, but it may well be that doing so is a key to improvement. This is an example of what we mean by "keeping it real"—confronting one's issue head-on and dealing with it, rather than essentially burying one's head in the sand and trying to convince oneself that the issue, whatever it is, isn't really out there.

As was the case with this leader, many leaders we have worked with over the years have said something along the lines of, "I figured I would see that in my 360" or "I've heard that many times before." One specific value to having an expert, such as a skilled coach or manager, work to help a leader decipher his or her 360-degree feedback is the fact that—among other things—the coach can point out data or comments in the feedback that drive home a point in order to clarify the importance of hearing the same feedback for the umpteenth time.

In addition to creating a more accurate sense of what one is actually good and not so good at, greater self-awareness among our most improved leaders also led to increased levels of motivation that perhaps would not have been realized. It is almost as if the 360-degree feedback was an incentive to better leverage one's strengths and/or address one's areas for development because of the weight leaders assigned to the feedback. As one leader said, "I took my feedback to heart because I really want to be a better leader," adding that, "I was going through some soul-searching about my career and wondering if this was the place for me, and that made me open to the feedback."

This comment reflects a theme we have seen with numerous clients over the years: That leaders receiving feedback may experience the same feedback very differently depending on the timing and context. For example, one leader we worked with not too long ago indicated, "I have always heard this feedback (that I am too driven for results and that I 'run people over' in the process of getting to my goals), but I always shrugged it off because it never really 'hurt' me before."

However, this leader added that, "Now I am starting to worry that people may actually see me as a jerk, not just a result-focused guy—and I want to get results, but I don't want to be a jerk." This leader had heard similar feedback for 10-plus years, but only now was it resonating with him in a way that created pressure to actually do something about it. The timing and context had changed such that the same feedback had a different impact on his willingness to take action.

In summary, one theme we found among our most improved leaders was that they seemed to be wired in such a way that they genuinely welcomed the feedback and sincerely wanted to take advantage of the opportunity to learn about and better themselves. As one of our leaders put it, "Just the process of getting feedback and trying to better myself, and finding a better way, was a clear motivation."

Self-Improvement

Another theme we saw can best be described as an honest, growth-oriented desire for action. This meant that leaders took the awareness they gathered from the 360-degree feedback to the next level in order to drive action. One leader's detailed comment captures the essence of how self-awareness led to self-improvement:

> I think awareness is a key for me. If I'm aware of something, I can take action and improve it. So it's a matter of examining the good feedback vs. the areas of opportunity. Once I had that, it's just a natural process I go through in my mind that leads me to take action. I think to myself, "OK, now how do I get better?"

So while it may seem obvious that increasing self-awareness (in this case through a 360-degree feedback process) would increase the desire to change, it is not always the case. Any manager or Learning and Organizational Development professional out there can attest to the level of defensiveness, deflection, and argumentation that a leader receiving feedback can engage in. But while some leaders may not translate increased awareness into productive action, our research clearly indicates that the most improved leaders did in fact take the insights they learned through the 360-degree feedback process and turn that insight into actions for self-improvement.

Other leaders noted that openness to improving resulted in accountability. For these leaders, their tendencies toward growth resulted in commitment to action. For example, one leader shared that, "I think it really was the willingness to change and the accountability that led to my behavior change and improvement." This leader added that, "Meeting with somebody on a regular basis to get coaching kept it front and center, and letting my colleagues know I was involved in this put a little social pressure on me."

As we will discuss later, this idea of "letting people know" turns out to be a critical aspect of what our most improved leaders did that helped them actually get better during the process. The point here is that increased self-awareness for this leader allowed him to talk to others about his development areas and progress.

And just as important as accountability, directed effort played a role in self-improvement. Many of our most improved leaders acknowledged that their self-improvement was targeted to specific areas. This, of course, allowed them to be efficient and effective in their quest for improvement.

· For most of the leaders we work with, having focus on specific areas to improve upon is only (or mostly) a result of the awareness brought on by their 360-degree feedback. In other words, leaders often have some diffused sense of needing to improve, but they only have the clarity and focus they need to start engaging in new behaviors once they receive the specific feedback contained in a 360-degree feedback report. This clarity then leads them to focused action—to actually do something about their development needs—rather than just a thought or feeling about wanting to improve but not having enough specific focus to execute on their intentions.

An analogy may further clarify. Let's use driving a car as something most of us do regularly. Like leaders, many drivers think they are pretty good, even above average, at driving. Occasionally you may have the feeling that you could do better, but you are probably not self-aware enough to engage in any directed effort at self-improvement (after all, who goes to driving school unless they have to in order to avoid getting more points on their license?). Maybe you sometimes are reminded by a spouse, partner, or friend to "be a better driver," but that's not likely to trigger you to do anything differently.

Now, if 15 of your closest friends, family members, and neighbors all indicate that you: (1) drive too fast in the neighborhood and (2) frequently roll through the stops sign at the nearby four-way intersection, then this increased self-awareness would potentially trigger in you some directed effort to improve (for example, keeping in mind and adjusting behaviorally to drive 25 mph vs. 40 mph in the neighborhood, and being sure to come to a complete stop at the intersection). In other words, feedback leads to self-awareness, which leads to directed action—whether you are trying to improve your driving skills or your leadership performance.

Authenticity with Others

Follow-up

In addition to demonstrating self-awareness and self-improvement, our most improved leaders went beyond keeping it real with themselves and extended that mindset to others. That is, they not only recognized their feedback and need to improve within their own minds, but they took action to be authentic with others about their development—thus keeping it real with their colleagues, teams, and other stakeholders.

Of note, leaders often followed up with feedback providers right after receiving their feedback. Many of the leaders in our "How Leaders Improve" sample thanked stakeholders who had given them feedback—either by e-mail or a quick phone call or by talking directly with those they see on a regular basis. Many of them also used this conversation to solicit ongoing feedback from these same individuals (for example, asking them to "keep me honest" and suggesting that others "let me know if you see it working"), thus demonstrating a public commitment to growth and improvement.

Indeed, previous research has indicated that managers who follow up with feedback providers after 360 assessments tend to improve in their performance.[1] And in fact, one of the leaders we worked with shared that immediately after receiving her feedback, she reached out and explained what the next steps would be. As she put it, "I sent a note to everyone to say thank you, and told them how I was going to use the feedback. I also committed to my management team that 'I am going to do this.'"

Our research indicated that follow-up not only demonstrates appreciation for and value associated with the feedback, but it also holds leaders accountable and involves others in the development process. To illustrate, one leader in our sample explained how she directly sought input from her direct reports via follow-up: "Also, I told my direct reports that I was committed to continuing to meet with them on this, and I asked them to call me out on it if I was not following through. That helped them to keep me honest."

Indeed, we often counsel leaders to give people permission to offer real-time feedback, as we know from experience that colleagues often observe leadership behaviors that could be improved but hesitate to share it with the leader. Thus, asking your team (or other colleagues) to keep you honest is a simple, straightforward way to give people that kind of permission. There are a variety of ways in which you can specifically tell people you are open to their ongoing feedback and input, but the underlying goal is the same: to indicate openness to *future* feedback by showing appreciation for the current feedback.

There is something very powerful about appreciating others' commitment to helping us succeed. Leaders going out of their way to show appreciation for the time and effort others took to provide feedback during a developmental process may seem like such a small act of graciousness, yet we consistently see how grateful those colleagues are for having been told "thank you" in some form or another. Maybe the novelty of being appreciated will eventually wear off—if all leaders would practice this habit of thanking those who have provided feedback during a 360 process—but we have a strong feeling that human nature will prevail and colleagues will feel perpetually underappreciated, thus continuing to make the simple act of following up to thank colleagues who participated in the process a huge positive in the eyes of those very colleagues.

Transparency

After following up with feedback providers, our most improved leaders took the opportunity to openly disclose their development plans, or what they were specifically doing to improve, with others. Again, this approach likely generated a recognition and respect for leaders' efforts and is something we have consistently seen as a powerful mechanism for positively influencing the views of stakeholders of any given leader. As one leader shared:

> After we completed the 360, I did circle back with people who completed the survey. I did it either in-person or by email. I shared with them that "these were the themes and the things I would be working on." That way, they knew what the feedback was, and that those areas were chosen for a reason, which gave people context.

As one leader insightfully recognized, when you share with others what you are purposefully striving for, they will notice (provided you are showing efforts and positive results!). So transparency about the leaders' specific areas for improvement and action steps gives others the opportunity to notice positive changes.

When reflecting on what helped with the change process during the post-360-degree feedback period, one leader noted: "Probably two things. First, the fact that I took the issues that I wanted to work on, both from a developmental perspective and from a strengths perspective, seriously. Also, being very transparent about what I was working on, because if people know you are working on things, they'll notice improvements." The fact that others are more likely to pay attention to any changes that a leader makes if they have been told about that leader's intentions of specifically focusing on changing that behavior is not new to many leadership development professionals, including these authors. We have consistently seen the value in giving stakeholders a heads-up on what a leader might be working on—if for no other reason than to ensure that when the leader makes that change, it registers in the mind of the stakeholder.

And what was more interesting was that leaders' authenticity likely inspired others to develop and improve. Naturally, development had a ripple and cyclical effect on others, resulting in organizational growth. So, as one leader said, the evolution she was experiencing as a result of the feedback resulted in an evolution of others as well: "The feedback from my team was useful and inspired me to change, which also created change in them. I saw an evolution in several of them taking more responsibility (as I elevated my focus to a higher level). So when I changed, they changed too."

We would add that in this area, leaders also varied in terms of how much they decided to disclose about their development plans. Depending on the leader, there were varying levels of transparency. However, many of the most improved leaders did follow-up with feedback providers to thank them and disclose the areas of focus. Some leaders were completely open about their process, such as the leader who said:

> I went back to my direct reports and shared my feedback and action plan. But that's consistent with how open I always was with them. I told them I appreciated the feedback, and that I was going to be working on some things. I did this as a group, and it went really well. Their response was, "Hey, it's great you are in this leadership program, and that you are taking our thoughts into consideration regarding how you are managing us."

And alternatively, one leader exhibited thoughtfulness about how much to share while also recognizing the importance of transparency:

> After the feedback I talked with my direct reports—some 1:1, and some in meetings—but only when it made sense. I didn't make it an agenda item in a team meeting, but I did discuss it—more organically. That was the most natural way for me. I don't try to hide anything or pretend that I don't have areas to work on, but you need to be careful about not losing credibility. I felt like I needed to be mindful of how I went about doing this.

This line of thinking may represent a more conservative approach to being transparent, and we see this often in our work—but it still captures the spirit (and behavior) of transparency that we noticed in our research. Sharing with others, even if you are thoughtful and considered in what and how you share, can gain the advantages that come along with this leadership practice. And while we find that many leaders have some hesitation about being transparent about their developmental feedback—typically because they feel that it will lower their perceived competence—our experience overwhelmingly points to a net positive experience.

While oversharing is possible, and there may be circumstances in which sharing this kind of information may not be prudent, in our experience, such situations are by far the exception and not the rule. More often than not, we counsel leaders to push past their discomfort at showing vulnerability and indeed share some of their feedback (and thoughts about that feedback, especially any specific plans to address it) with others, which almost always results in the positive benefits of increased credibility, trust, and openness that so many leaders hope to achieve in the eyes of their colleagues, bosses, and direct reports.

So, while the level of transparency may have varied between some of our most improved leaders, they all engaged in some type of follow-up and transparent communication about what they were working on with at least some of their key stakeholders. This finding in our research, that there is a positive impact when leaders engage others specifically by sharing their feedback (and plan of action) during a developmental experience, is an important one, but not a surprising one to us. By openly communicating their feedback and learning during the process (aka, keeping it real) leaders strongly reinforce what we have seen in our own practice—that being transparent boosts internal commitment within the leader and sets up stakeholders to be ready to view that leader differently going forward.

In summary, among the leaders who tend to get the best results out of their development experiences, we find the same dynamic: By engaging in conversations with others and sharing some aspect of their feedback (and usually also the resulting developmental goals), leaders create a perception of commitment, openness, and self-awareness. These perceptions then further leaders' goals by making those they lead and work with more likely to see them differently (and in a better light), which in turn positively impacts their perceived effectiveness as leaders.

Recommendations

For the Leader

- Be honest with yourself about your strengths and weaknesses; it may be painful to acknowledge faults (or humbling to reflect on how others view your strengths), but successful leadership development starts with staring the truth in the face and deciding to deal with it.
- Be candid with others—you don't have to self-immolate in front of your stakeholders, but you should own up to your shortcomings and what you plan to do to improve.
- When you disagree with some feedback or feel defensive about a message you have received, consider whether the same message would be received

differently by you if your closest friend or ally were delivering it (usually we see ill-intent in negative feedback, but if someone we trust gave us the same message, we would be more open to it and tend to believe them).

- Overcome the fear of revealing your weaknesses to others—they already know about them! Talking about them won't make them true or untrue, it will just give you a chance to demonstrate your willingness to address them and will enhance your reputation as a courageous, committed leader.
- Interpret the feedback from the most positive assumed intent (if I consider this feedback was truly meant to help me, how would I interpret it?).
- Be clear about how you are interpreting the feedback, ask people to confirm that your interpretation is valid, and commit to working on it.
- Check in with people to see whether they are seeing you working on your plan, and whether the actions are having an observable impact.

For the Organization

- Understand the natural human elements that prevent people from openly discussing their development needs and development plans—and then also look at what the organizational culture (and senior leaders in particular) are doing to either support, or avoid, honest dialogue about self-improvement as leaders.
- Build time and forums for sharing feedback and action plans.
- Recognize people who are good role models for receiving and acting on feedback.

For the Coach

- Be ready to overcome resistance in leaders you coach—not just resistance to feedback or specific development areas—but also resistance to the idea of publicly discussing shortcomings and development issues.
- Have the evidence (research-based and anecdotal) ready to convince clients of the benefit of being candid with themselves and with others, and be ready to make specific recommendations about *how* they can discuss their development with others.
- Empathize with the natural fears that leaders have about opening themselves up to their colleagues about development areas. Doing so is not without risk; therefore, you should demonstrate that you understand the tension between being open and fearing judgment or consequences by discussing both sides of the equation (both pros and cons about being honest with others).
- Encourage appropriate vulnerability for leaders.
- Be as concrete as possible with what good focus looks like.

CHAPTER ELEVEN

Focus on Strengths . . . and Weaknesses

We sometimes note when working with groups of leaders that there "isn't that much that is new under the sun" when it comes to leadership effectiveness. Occasionally, however, there is a shift in the field of leadership development that is truly groundbreaking. We believe that such a shift occurred around the year 2000.

Up until that point, our basic approach to leadership development was as follows. We would gather 360-degree feedback on some leaders, then work with those leaders individually to help each one develop an action plan. The typical action plan consisted of a table with three columns: one for strengths, one for areas for development, and one for action steps.

The areas for development invariably dealt with a leader's lower-rated survey items and critical written comments from the 360-degree report. And the action steps invariably dealt with the leader's areas for development. We followed this approach for years without giving it so much as a second thought.

Then, between 1999 and 2003, several books appeared in the popular business press that changed the way many of us think about and practice leadership development. In particular, these books caused us to rethink our approach to action planning when working with leaders. Among the groundbreaking books were *The Extraordinary Leader* by Zenger and Folkman[1] and *First, Break All the Rules* by Buckingham and Coffman.[2]

These authors had done some research suggesting that instead of helping leaders identify action steps to aid them in addressing relative weaknesses (meaning areas for development related to lower-rated 360-degree feedback items and critical written comments), a better approach to developing leaders might involve helping them to get even better in areas in which they were already strong. This represented a paradigm shift in the field of leadership, resulting in new tools such as the popular Strengths Finder self-assessment developed by Tom Rath of the Gallup organization.[3]

The paradigm shift toward leveraging strengths in the leadership development space was reflective of the broader positive psychology zeitgeist of the time, led by luminaries such as Martin Seligman and Mihály Csíkszentmihályi. This movement emphasized that therapy in particular, and psychology in general, did not necessarily need to focus exclusively on deficits, sickness, or dysfunction. Instead, the positive psychology movement emphasized the study of strengths that enable individuals and communities to thrive.

This paradigm shift also changed the way we approach action planning with the leaders we work with. No longer is it simply assumed that one's developmental actions should be related to lower-rated items and more critical written comments in a 360-degree report. Rather, we now explore with leaders the question of whether they should be working on addressing relative weaknesses, or whether they should be working on better leveraging existing strengths (and/or seeking to turn "strengths" into "spikes," meaning areas in which one is not merely strong, but rather extraordinary). It is our experience that individuals find leveraging strengths to be more inspirational than improving on weaknesses, and there are at least some who believe that people can actually make greater progress in more fully leveraging an existing strength than they can in rectifying true developmental areas.

Just helping leaders to fully grasp that it is legitimate and important to focus on building on strengths is critical. As one leader put it, "What I remember about when I had my first meeting with my leadership coach is that I had more positive than negative areas, and he coached me through the idea that it's just as important to build on strengths."

Strengths and Weaknesses—Not Either/Or

We believe it is possible to err too far in either direction—focusing only on strengths or only on weaknesses. In general, our most improved leaders sought to both build on strengths and to address relative weaknesses. As one leader put it, "I worked on both strengths and weaknesses, but my action plan was skewed more toward strengths."

In some cases, an area for improvement was seen as a strength, but with some relative weaknesses embedded within the strength. As one leader put it, "Relationship Building was a strength, but I also had some opportunity areas in that area, such as giving and receiving feedback, so I embedded some relative weaknesses within my strengths."

Another leader cited a similar example: "Communication came out as a strength in my feedback, but there was an aspect of communication that my feedback suggested I needed to improve at, and that was visibility and presence." Similarly, this leader had strength in the area of building talent but said it was clear he needed to work on aligning goals when developing people. In the end, this leader concluded that his action plan was probably "more focused on areas for improvement."

It's amazing to us how often our most improved leaders used the term *confidence* in our interviews. It has caused us to realize that often what a leader needs more than new leadership skills is just a higher degree of confidence that he or she has great leadership skills, and the key is going in to work each day feeling confident. We have come to believe that many of the sorts of skills that we attempt to teach leaders in our leadership development programs, in areas such as leadership presence and upward influence, will almost naturally flow from higher levels of self-confidence, provided that such confidence is well validated by one's feedback.

The initial coaching session with one of our most improved leaders illustrates this. She recounted that, "because of my 360 feedback, it was hard to find any real weaknesses, so we ended up deciding to include two strengths and one area for development in my action plan. I liked the fact that it was a combination of the two, because it's confidence boosting to focus on strengths."

Who Improves the Most?

For purposes of the current study, an obvious question to wrestle with was: Did the leaders who improved the most focus more on addressing relative weaknesses, or did they focus more on better leveraging strengths (and/or turning strengths into spikes)?

The single most common word that we heard in response to the interview question about whether one's action plan involved building on strengths or addressing relative weaknesses was *combination*. And, even when interviewees did not use that very word, they often used similar ways of getting at the same idea, such as the phrase that one's action plan was "evenly split" between strengths and relative weaknesses. So, while we acknowledge that the "old school" approach of focusing just on weaknesses is not the ideal approach to developing leaders, we have also concluded that one can allow the pendulum to swing too far in the direction of just building on strengths.

At the same time, some of our most improved leaders clearly focused more on either strengths or relative weaknesses. As one leader put it, "my plan leaned more toward building on strengths," while another said "my actions were geared toward addressing relative weaknesses." So, while we are generally supportive of the move over the past several years toward more of a strengths-based approach to leadership development, what we have learned from our most improved leaders is that there is no single formula here: Some focus on strengths, some focus on weaknesses, and some focus on a combination of the two.

Of course, this prompts the question: How does a leader determine which way to go on this? We believe that the answer, at least in part, is based a key insight discussed in an earlier chapter: the importance of focusing on a central issue. Quite simply, when we probed why our most improved leaders chose to focus on building on strengths, addressing relative weaknesses, or a combination of the two, the most common response was that the decision was based on what one's central issue was, more so than the question of whether one's key areas for development were best labeled "strengths" or "areas for development."

One of our most improved leaders illustrated this insight by stating that her action plan included "a combination of my strengths and my weaknesses," but that most of her specific action steps dealt more with her relative weaknesses, because "I thought they were related more to my central issue." In this case, the leader's central issue was empowerment—or, in the leader's words, the idea that she had to empower her team to "own their areas of the business" and take more accountability for them. "This," she said, "was front of mind—everything pointed to that."

We think that last phrase—"everything pointed to that"—is a key statement, because it gets at the essence of what a central issue is. And sometimes, the data that points to a given leadership competency as one's central issue involves both strengths that can be better leveraged as well as relative weaknesses that should be addressed.

In fact, a review of the action plan this leader developed in response to her feedback indicated that she was very strategic and had a great drive for results, but that she also was seen as needing to be more flexible in terms of how her people approached issues. When she added all of this up, it pointed to the idea of needing to be better able to empower others: To be flexible in terms of how her direct reports approached things, to hold them accountable for results, and to thus free herself up to focus more on what she was naturally strong at and what she was expected to excel at as the leader of a function within her organization—strategic leadership.

As leadership coaches, there was a time when we didn't really know what to do with a 360 report in which all the scores were strong.

Sometimes these ended up being very short coaching sessions, because the message was basically "It looks like you are doing a great job—just keep it up." Now, however, when confronted with leaders who have really strong feedback, we treat those coaching sessions quite differently.

What It Means to Leverage Strengths

The phrase "leverage a strength" has become very popular in the field of leadership development over the past several years, but we don't think the phrase is necessarily self-explanatory. So one thing we have sought to do when coaching leaders is to provide guidance on exactly what it means to leverage a strength.

One of the authors collaborated with a peer in writing an article for *T+D* on how leaders can leverage their strengths ("Focus on Your Strengths").[4] In this article, the authors posited that it would be irresponsible to focus development exclusively on either strengths or weaknesses and that the recommended approach is to balance focusing on strengths with addressing weaknesses. In addition, the authors highlighted four specific ways in which an individual can more fully leverage his or her strengths. In reviewing our interview notes from our most improved leaders, we were pleased to see that each of the four strategies highlighted in the article was described independently by our sample of leaders.

One example of what it means to "leverage a strength" is to simply do more of something that a leader already does quite well. To illustrate, one of our most improved leaders described how "networking was a strength of mine, but I needed to do more of it, and I needed a *reason* or *purpose* for doing it more." So this leader's action plan involved having a series of conversations with key colleagues for the purpose of finding out more about those colleagues and the parts of the business in which they worked. This leader explained that the business project that was part of the development program she went through also served as a good conversation starter. This example illustrates not only what it means to leverage a strength, but also how a leadership development program can create opportunities for conversations that might not otherwise happen.

Another way one can leverage a strength is to use this skill to counteract or address a weakness. This is reflected in a comment from one of our most improved leaders: "I remember that my leadership coach asked me to not just look at weaknesses but to try to leverage strengths in order to help improve the weaknesses." This leader had excellent feedback in the area of communicating openly, but got feedback that he was relatively weak at active listening. The key for this leader was to think of open communication as a two-way street and to realize that he was only driving in one direction. By seeking to open up the flow of communication in *each* direction, he was able to use a strength to help address a weakness.

A third way one can leverage a strength is to spread the strength, by teaching it to others. This can be done through mentoring programs, formal management of team members, or even leading internal skill-building sessions on a topic. An example comes to mind of an individual we worked with. This individual was considered one of the premier strategic thinkers in his organization. His company was investing heavily in a leadership development initiative. One of the elements the organization wanted to address in this leadership development initiative was to enhance the strategic thinking skills of their managers, who were generally thought to be far better executors than strategic thinkers who spent time anticipating industry trends. The leader was asked to lead sessions on practical steps that director-level talent could engage in to think and lead more strategically. These sessions were exceptionally well received by participants, in part because of the credibility of the source and also because of the actionability of the recommendations he offered.

Finally, leveraging a strength sometimes means seeking to build a strength into a spike. The prestigious management consulting firm McKinsey & Company collaborated with Egon Zehnder on a research-based article in 2011 entitled *Return on Leadership—Competencies that Generate Growth.*[5] This article encouraged organizations to develop and promote "spiky leaders." Their research highlighted a strong correlation between revenue growth and leaders who had clear spikes (that is, well-developed strengths), even if they demonstrated underperformance in other leadership dimensions. They suggested that organizations should help leaders to "build on their brilliance, just as much as it must help them to address their deficiencies."

Some of our favorite leadership development authors, Jack Zenger and Joe Folkman, also published research that both established criteria for what constitutes a spike and also made a compelling quantitative case for the importance of a leader developing spikes.[6] The criterion that Zenger and Folkman used to determine what constitutes a spike is that it refers to a competency in which an individual is at or above the 90th percentile when compared with his or her peers (or, put differently, a competency in which one is in the top 10%).

The compelling case that Zenger and Folkman made for the importance of leaders being at or above the 90th percentile in one or more areas was based on their analysis of a very large data set of 360-degree feedback. Specifically, they looked at the relationship between the number of spikes a given leader has and his or her overall perceived effectiveness. They found that if a leader has no spikes whatsoever, that leader falls at the 34th percentile in terms of overall leader effectiveness. If a leader has one spike, on the other hand, that leader falls at the 64th percentile in terms of overall leader effectiveness.

In other words, if a leader has zero spikes, then instead of focusing on a relative weakness that is likely never going to be a spike for that leader (given his or her unique personality, interests, and so on), that leader may be better off seeking to develop at least one area in which he or she is relatively strong into a single spike. Moreover, Zenger and Folkman found that the leader who has four spikes falls at the 89th percentile in terms of overall perceived effectiveness—meaning right at the cusp of being in the top 10% overall.

Since being exposed to the excellent research done by Zenger and Folkman (as well as other authors doing great work in the same area), we have done a couple of things differently. First, when designing our 360-degree feedback instruments, we generally include a column in the feedback report that shows the leader receiving the feedback on how he or she compares to his or her colleagues, competency by competency and survey item by survey item. More specifically, our standard 360-degree report format has built into it some ways of clearly indicating survey competencies and items for which a given leader is already at or above the 90th percentile, as well as the size of the gap in areas where the leader has fallen short of that lofty standard.

The other thing we do differently since reading the Zenger and Folkman research is that, in our early coaching conversations with leaders we are working with, we explore the question of whether there are areas in one's report where a leader appears to be within striking distance of having a spike. For example, if a leader is at the 80th percentile for a competency in which he or she also has some natural giftedness and some passion, and where there is a clear organizational need, we may encourage that leader to develop an action plan that may help the leader move from the 80th percentile to the 90th percentile or greater in that area. In other words, we encourage the leader to turn a strength into a spike.

Based on our interview data, the idea of turning strengths into spikes was, at a minimum, a memorable and thought-provoking idea. As one of our most improved leaders put it, "the aspect of the training program I most recall is the concept of spikes, and focusing on building strengths into spikes." This leader further recalled that, "if you have a certain number of spikes, people will focus more on those than they will on weaknesses, provided the weaknesses are relatively mild." This is a very good paraphrase of what the leaders we work with learn about the relationship between strengths, spikes, and relative weaknesses.

Zenger and Folkman provide practical suggestions on when to focus on strengths versus weaknesses. As mentioned above, their research suggests that "jacks of all trades" (for example, those who are pretty good at a wide range of leadership skills but true masters of none) do not tend to be perceived as highly effective leaders. They encourage these leaders to invest in building on their strengths. However, they also noted that some leaders have development areas that could potentially derail their careers. They provide the logical recommendation that these leaders should focus on addressing their "derailer" areas of weakness before turning to more fully leveraging their strengths. While the question of how much to focus on strengths versus relative weaknesses remains fertile ground for additional research among leadership development professionals, we hope this book adds to the knowledge in this area. Quite simply, our most improved leaders, as a whole, focused on both—rather than allowing the pendulum to swing too far in one direction or the other.

Recommendations

For the Leader

- Identify the source of your strengths. When you repeatedly get positive affirmation for a particular behavior or action, reflect on what it is that you're doing differently than others that accounts for these successes. Focus more on the unique way you're approaching the task rather than on the successful outcome itself.

- Once you've triangulated the source of the differentiating strength, explore (either via reflection or discussion with others) how you might deploy this strength in new or different ways. What challenges is your team, department, or organization facing? How could your particular spike be of benefit in these areas?

- Consider which strengths are most important to future success, and double down on those.

- Once you've identified your strengths or even your spikes (areas where you are at or above the 90th percentile), ask yourself what "even better" would look like.

- Learn about what individuals who are even better than you are do. In other words, if you are a great motivator, identify individual leaders who are even better than you in this area and seek to adopt some of their best practices.

- Ensure you have identified some action steps to leverage strengths. For example, explore whether you can use a strength of yours to address developmental areas. At the very least, ensure that at least one action item is related to strengths-based development.

For the Organization

- Create internal mentoring groups led by your best-in-class leaders in certain skill areas. In other words, if you are looking to develop strategic thinking skills, have your most highly rated strategic thinkers invest time in upgrading the—skills of their colleagues. They will likely enjoy the experience and be excellent teachers.

- Create a culture that recognizes and celebrates strengths. Teach your people managers to focus on developing strengths. Most individuals are reticent about focusing on developing strengths when their managers are constantly emphasizing a deficit-based model of development. Managers need to understand the rationale and potential ROI of strengths-based development.

- Use strengths to help determine who gets what extra development (training, assignments, etc.).

- Create a culture that recognizes and celebrates strengths.

For the Coach

- When a leader is getting very positive feedback in a particular area, spend time focusing in on what the leader does that accounts for this success (the "active ingredient"). The behavior is likely second nature to the leader, and, in our experience, leaders tend to be more focused on the positive outcomes than on the component steps or skills that result in the positive outcome. Awareness around their true differentiators may help them to think about how they can deploy these differentiators more fully.

- Guard against the tendency for leaders to want to focus only on their weaknesses. Force the conversation and the planning to address what else can be done to further a leader's strengths. The most important thing a coach can do regarding strengths-based development is to emphasize it to some degree in the action planning process.

CHAPTER TWELVE

Where We've Been and Where We're Going

Our research with leaders who have improved greatly has illustrated a number of important concepts that can help individuals and organizations to fully realize a return on their leadership development efforts. Although there are countless books on what good leadership looks like, there are precious few resources available that explore and explain how leaders actually improve and sustain this improvement over an extended period of time. What any experienced manager or leadership development professional can tell you is that simply offering someone a sage piece of advice about what to do differently does not correlate well with sustained change. The research highlighted in this book bridges this implementation and sustainability gap between having a good idea for improvement and actually making the improvement.

At the conclusion of each of our 10 "Insights" chapters, we have offered three sets of recommendations about how to deploy the insights based on the three audiences for whom we have written this book. First, we think this book is a valuable resource for leaders who are looking to improve themselves in a meaningful and sustainable manner. Second, we think Learning & Organizational Development professionals would benefit from incorporating the insights highlighted throughout the book into their efforts to develop leaders. Finally, we believe this book represents a valuable resource for those individuals who are responsible for helping others develop or improve upon their skill sets. At a minimum, this would include managers who are working to improve the skills of their direct reports and executive coaches/consultants who are hired to help individuals grow and develop.

One tool we believe will be beneficial to all three of these audiences is the RIPEN assessment that we have developed. This assessment was designed to support individuals, coaches, and organizations in their efforts to develop others. Specifically, once an individual has identified a development goal (after a 360 process, or perhaps more commonly after a performance review), individuals can complete the RIPEN assessment to assess internal and external factors on the five elements of the RIPEN model (Readiness, Incentive, Pressure, Expectation, and Natural Inclination). The results of this assessment are very informative in identifying either who is likely to be a good candidate for a development initiative or how to focus or structure a coaching engagement in order to realize the desired ROI from the engagement. Please contact Avion Consulting at info@avionconsulting.com for more information on this assessment.

At a high level, we believe there are four major themes highlighted throughout this book. First, we explore the conditions that cause individuals to be ready to make a change. Some of these conditions are internal to the individual looking to make a change (internal ripeness factors); others are ways in which the environment influences leaders to be more or less ripe for change. It is our belief that the external factors matter only insomuch as they impact the appropriate internal ripeness factors. Thus, identifying where someone needs to ripen should influence the nature of external influences offered (for example, feedback, time, carrots and sticks, urgency drivers, confidence-building, or safety-netting).

In other words, providing great advice is not likely to be impactful to someone who lacks the incentive to change. It is our experience that most coaches and managers try to influence people in the way with which they are most familiar. Given the complexity of behavior change, this is not surprising. However, we hope this book will help the reader better identify and assess what levers one needs to pull in order to support specific individuals in their development.

A second cluster of insights we explore in this book focuses on the attributes of the development areas selected by our most improved leaders. Specifically, central issue, penetrating message, and guiding metaphor are all insights that relate to the topic on which an individual decides to focus his or her action planning. Essentially, these insights are different avenues that created memorability and focus for our most improved leaders (consistency of message, emotional impact of message, and using a metaphor to remind oneself of an area of focus).

Coaches, leaders, and organizations are well served to incorporate reflection on these three topics into their action planning process (What is your central issue? What penetrating message did you take from your feedback?

What guiding metaphor will you use in thinking about your evolution as a leader?).

Third, we offer a set of insights regarding the attributes of leadership development programs that appeared to promote meaningful progress for our most improved leaders. Specifically, our data suggest that involving others, crafting a well-structured training experience, critical conversations, and keeping it real are all important elements of the training program itself that were cited as yielding beneficial outcomes.

Finally, we share the insight that, while the trend in the field of leadership development at the time of our study is to focus on strengths-based development, our most improved leaders actually focused on a combination of building on strengths and addressing relative weaknesses in their efforts to get better as leaders. So, while we continue to encourage the leaders we work with to reflect on their strengths and think about how to best leverage them, our research has caused us to conclude that the pendulum may have swung too far in the direction of strengths-based development, and we are encouraging the leaders we work with to really think through the optimal combination of strengths and relative weaknesses with regard to areas of focus when seeking to improve.

In order to build on the research on which this book is based, there are at least three additional analyses we recommend. First, as mentioned throughout this book, the majority of the leaders in our study were participating in a high-potential program. In other words, we have drawn our insights largely from already high-performing leaders. It is possible that if we were to utilize the same methodology with a more "normally distributed population" of leaders (for example, including A, B, and C players in our population) we would find new, different, or unique insights. In several instances throughout the book we have speculated about where we believe this is likely. However, it is entirely possible that there are plenty of other differences that would emerge upon conducting this analysis.

As referenced earlier in this book, our company, Avion Consulting, helps take individual leaders, teams, and organizations to new heights. This book represents a deep dive into how individual leaders improve. In the future, we also intend to conduct similar analyses on how teams improve and how organizations improve. The same gaps in the literature that we noted at the outset of this book exist regarding how teams and organizations improve. For example, there is a fair amount of research and perspective on the attributes of high-performing teams, but very little on how teams in an organizational context actually improve their effectiveness.

The same can be said for organizational effectiveness. The literature on organizational health is robust, and there are many sophisticated and well-researched measures of organizational health that we and other consulting firms utilize. However, we continue to be surprised that there is not a great deal of research available that explains why some organizations make the transition from having moderately engaging environments to having highly engaging environments, while others continue to operate at suboptimal levels. These areas represent future avenues of research Avion Consulting intends to explore, and we look forward to sharing our insights with you.

Notes

Chapter 1

1. Jeffery Pfeffer, *Getting Beyond the BS in Leadership Literature* (McKinsey Quarterly, January 2016).

2. Jim Collins, *Good to Great: Why Some Companies Make the Leap . . . and Others Don't* (New York: Harper Business, 2011).

3. James L. Heskett, W. Earl Sasser, and Leonard Schlesinger, *The Service Profit Chain: How Leading Companies Link Profit and Growth to Loyalty, Satisfaction, and Value* (New York: The Free Press, 1997).

4. John Zenger and Joseph Folkman, *The Extraordinary Leader: Turning Good Managers into Great Leaders* (New York: McGraw-Hill, 2002).

5. Marcus Buckingham and Curt Coffman, *First, Break All the Rules: What the World's Greatest Managers Do Differently* (New York: Simon & Schuster, 1999).

Chapter 2

1. Lao Tzu, *Tao Te Ching* (New York: Vintage Books, 1972).

2. James Prochaska and Carlo DiClemente, "The transtheoretical approach," in J. C. Norcross and M. R. Goldfried, eds. *Handbook of Psychotherapy Integration, 2nd ed.* (New York: Oxford University Press; 2005), 147–171.

3. Albert Bandura, *Self-efficacy: The Exercise of Control* (New York: Freeman, 1997).

4. Carol S. Dweck, *Mindset: The New Psychology of Success* (New York: Random House, 2006).

Chapter 3

1. Towers Watson, Change and Communication ROI—The 10th Anniversary Report: How the Fundamentals Have Evolved and the Best Adapt (New York: Towers Watson, 2013).

Chapter 4

1. Joseph Luft and Harrington Ingham, "The Johari window, a graphic model of interpersonal awareness," *Proceedings of the western training laboratory in group development* (Los Angeles: University of California, Los Angeles, 1955).

2. Leon Festinger, *A Theory of Cognitive Dissonance* (Evanston: Row, Peterson, 1957).

3. Albert Bandura, *Self-efficacy: The Exercise of Control* (New York: Freeman, 1997).

4. Daniel Goleman, *Emotional Intelligence: Why It Can Matter More Than IQ* (New York: Bantam Books, 1995).

Chapter 5

1. Leon Festinger, *A Theory of Cognitive Dissonance* (Evanston: Row, Peterson, 1957).

2. Aristotle, *Rhetoric* (Mineola: Dover Thrifts Editions, 2004), 106.

3. David Baldwin and Curt Grayson, *Influence: Gaining Commitment, Getting Results* (Center for Creative Leadership, 2004).

Chapter 7

1. Frances Hesselbein, Marshall Goldsmith, and Richard Beckhard, eds., *The Leader of the Future: New Visions, Strategies and Practices for the Next Era* (San Francisco: Jossey-Bass, 1997).

2. Jim Collins, *Good to Great: Why Some Companies Make the Leap . . . and Others Don't* (New York: Harper Business, 2001).

Chapter 8

1. Paul Hersey, Kenneth Blanchard, and Dewey Johnson, *Management of Organizational Behavior: Utilizing Human Resources* (Upper Saddle River, NJ: Prentice Hall, 1996).

Chapter 9

1. Michael O'Donnell, *Health Promotion in the Workplace,* 4th ed. (New York: Delmar, 2002).

2. Shelley Taylor, "Social Support: A Review," in M.S. Friedman, *The Handbook of Health Psychology* (New York: Oxford University Press, 2011), 189–214.

3. Manuel Barrera, "Distinctions between Social Support Concepts, Measures, and Models" (*American Journal of Community Psychology:* 14 (4), 1986), 413–445.

4. Thomas Ashby Wills and Margaret Clark, eds., *"Social Support and Interpersonal Relationships"* (*Prosocial Behavior, Review of Personality and Social Psychology:* 12, 1991), 265–289.

Chapter 10

1. Alan G. Walker and James W. Smither, A Five-Year Study of Upward Feedback: What Managers Do with Their Results Matters (*Personnel Psychology*, June, 1999).

Chapter 11

1. John Zenger and Joseph Folkman, *The Extraordinary Leader: Turning Good Managers into Great Leaders* (New York: McGraw-Hill, 2002).

2. Marcus Buckingham and Curt Coffman, *First, Break All the Rules: What the World's Greatest Managers Do Differently* (New York: Simon & Schuster, 1999).

3. Tom Rath, *StrengthsFinder 2.0* (Gallup Press, 2007).

4. Sacha Lindekens and Raluca Graebbner, "Focus on Your Strengths" (*T+D*, Vol. 68 (5) 2014), 70–74.

5. Asmus Komm, John McPherson, Magnus Graf Lambsdorff, Stephen P. Kelner, Jr., and Verena Renze-Westendorf, *Return on Leadership—Competencies That Generate Growth*" (New York: Egon Zehnder International and McKinsey & Company, 2011).

6. John Zenger and Joseph Folkman, *The Extraordinary Leader: Turning Good Managers into Great Leaders* (New York: McGraw-Hill, 2002).

Index

About the Authors

John Gates, PhD, is a Partner with Avion Consulting, a management consulting firm specializing in leadership, team, and organizational development. With more than 20 years of experience, Dr. Gates has coached and trained thousands of leaders around the world. Dr. Gates's areas of expertise include leadership effectiveness, coaching, communication, employee engagement, strategic planning, team building, and change management. Dr. Gates provides coaching and counsel to leaders from the middle management to senior executive levels; he partners with clients in the design and implementation of high-impact leadership development solutions; and he works with management teams on issues related to both team and organizational effectiveness. Dr. Gates also has extensive experience in the area of organizational assessment and follow-up, and he has helped numerous organizations achieve significant increases in leader credibility and employee engagement.

Dr. Gates has served clients in a wide range of industries, including financial services, healthcare, higher education, hospitality, retail, and many others. In addition to Dr. Gates's extensive experience as a management consultant, he has also served in both faculty and leadership positions at several universities, including California State University, Long Beach, and University of California, San Diego. Dr. Gates has a PhD in Communication Arts and Sciences from the University of Southern California.

Jeff Graddy, PhD, is a Partner with Avion Consulting whose passion is helping leaders get the best out of themselves and their people. He coaches senior executives and high-potential talent in order to maximize their impact on the business by focusing on their impact on people. Dr. Graddy also designs and leads innovative leadership development programs, specifically targeting the growth of future leaders who possess the emotional intelligence and influencing skills necessary to lead effectively in an increasingly dynamic, global context.

Dr. Graddy is honored to consult with a variety of premier organizations, including market leaders in healthcare, financial services, automotive, retail, technology, professional services, private equity, pharma, and not-for-profit. He takes pride in the long-term nature of his client relationships and the high impact achieved through those partnerships.

Dr. Graddy has been coaching senior leaders and building high-potential leadership programs for the past 13 years, reaching thousands of leaders all over the globe. Before his corporate consulting career, Dr. Graddy was in private practice as a sport psychology consultant, working with elite athletes and teams to help them leverage psychological principles for better performance. Dr. Graddy started his career in behavioral healthcare, serving both private and government sectors. He held clinical roles that ranged in focus from community mental health care to leading crisis response teams.

Dr. Graddy holds a PhD in Counseling Psychology from the University of Florida, where he also earned a Master's degree in Sport Psychology. He completed his doctoral residency at the University of San Diego. He is qualified to administer a range of psychological inventories and is a certified trainer in Emotional Intelligence. Dr. Graddy is also a member of the American Psychological Association's Society of Consulting Psychology and part of the International Society of Executive Coaching.

Sacha Lindekens, PhD, is a Partner with Avion Consulting who specializes in executive coaching and designing and delivering leadership development programs for organizations ranging from large multinational organizations to small to mid-sized family-owned entities. His client base is principally, but not exclusively, in the professional services, financial services, technology/media, and healthcare industries. Dr. Lindekens is a published author on the topic of executive coaching and leadership development, and he aspires to fill the role of trusted advisor with executives on their learning journey.

Dr. Lindekens has a particular interest in assisting leaders to deploy emotionally intelligent leadership. He consults with organizations to create robust leadership pipelines; attract, develop, and retain millennials; and enable executive teams to achieve their full potential. As a coach, he is known for his genuine tendency of being supportive, yet calling it the way he sees it.

Dr. Lindekens has been in the leadership consulting field for 15 years and has had a positive business impact on thousands of leaders across the globe. Prior to his consulting career, Dr. Lindekens was trained as a psychologist. He worked as a therapist, taught a variety of university-level courses, and assisted an NFL team in conducting psychological profiles on incoming rookies to determine their draftability and fit with the organization. Dr. Lindekens has led teams of consultants and researchers for 20 years. He has a track record of leading in a manner that yields both excellent business results and a strong team dynamic. Dr. Lindekens holds a PhD in Counseling Psychology from the University of Florida, an MEd in Counseling Psychology from Rutgers University, and a BA in Psychology from State University of New York, Albany.